The Happy Clam

Also by Rosemary Schmidt:

Go Forward, Support! The Rugby of Life

Rosebud's Blog:
www.RosebudsBlog.com
www.gainline.com
www.happyclam.net

Cover: Painting by Carol Aust, titled *Fearless*, acrylic on wood, photographed by Scot Langdon.

The Happy Clam

By

Rosemary A. Schmidt

GAINLINE PRESS
Watertown, Massachusetts

To Susan –
My rock, my harbor, love of my life, thank you for always
being there to pick me up when I am down –
'you raise me up'

Credits

Carol Aust's painting, titled *Fearless*, acrylic on wood, reproduced with the kind permission of the artist. Photographed by Scot Langdon of Long Hill Photography, a true professional in his craft.

Albert Einstein's quote reprinted with permission of the Albert Einstein Archives, The Hebrew University of Jerusalem

Eric C. Kintner's letter to the editor, published in *The Boston Globe* on Saturday, 29 April 2006, gratefully reprinted with the permission of the author.

General Colin L. Powell's (U.S. Army, Ret.) first rule of leadership, quoted at the 2015 Sage Summit, and in his book, *It Worked For Me*, shared with his permission.

A number of other brief quotes/excerpts are incorporated in the text in a transformative sense, and in the spirit of critical analysis, and believed to be consistent with Fair Use. There are many studies supporting the findings shared herein, and every effort has been made to reference the most relevant and original sources. Any omissions or errors are unintentional. The range of topics covered is so broad and multi-faceted, that this work can only scratch the tip of the iceberg. I myself have not read every work cover-to-cover. The interested reader is encouraged to seek out the original works.

Acknowledgments

I would like to thank the universe for all the encouragement and support from so many and so very unexpected corners. Thank you to:

Linda Francis, who encouraged me to start working on the next book, even if nothing came of the first one, when the first one was not even finished yet. Not your typical Citizens Bank banker!

Keith Elchert and Gayle Heiby Podczerwinski, and the rest of the editorial staff at the *Flyer News*, who took a chance on me, and gave me the opportunity to write a weekly column my senior year at the University of Dayton.

Brian McGrory at *The Boston Globe*, who read my letter to the editor, and encouraged me to start a blog and keep writing.

Nancy Etcoff, who encouraged me, and re-assured me there was certainly room in the world for another book on happiness.

Meghan Regan-Loomis, who edited the draft, and through her insights, challenged me to fill in the gaps, and truly helped in making this a better work.

Jenny Lemmons, my niece, who was along for the ride on most of this journey, and introduced me to Earl Gray (the tea).

Susan Lurier, who always sees and believes in "the god and poet" in me. And, I in you, my love.

Table of Contents

Recipes

Poems

There are going to be happy days and sorry days, and you have to learn to live with both.

Dad

If you want to make other people happy, you have to make yourself happy first.

Dad

You can't pour from an empty cup.

The Internet

A calm and modest life brings more happiness than the pursuit of success combined with constant restlessness.

Albert Einstein

You walk in here, and this is happiness. If you aren't happy in here, you don't know what happiness is.

Overheard at a bakery

Preface

I remember feeling left out. I've been that kid. Heck, I've been that grown-up. Eating lunch or going for a walk by myself. I've gotten used to it. I guess a person can get used to just about anything. When you get used to something good – that's called taking things for granted. That's not good. When you get used to something that's hard or bad, it's called adaptation, coping, or resiliency.

I've always felt lucky. Growing up with my older sister and knowing how tenuous her health was, I took nothing for granted. I knew I was lucky to have two legs, two lungs, and to be able to breathe.

Nothing in this life is guaranteed. Not life, not love, not any of it. Finding love, I took a few chances along the way, and I'm glad I did. Hard work, luck, fate, and opportunity, those are the four corners of this world, the points of our compass. We take our chances, and keep putting ourselves out there, and maybe things get a little better each day. If you read nothing else, and put this back on the bookshelf, remember this one thing alone: Things can get better.

The Crayon Poem

I'd like to travel
The lifespan
Of a crayon

All the hills and hollows
Before that first pen

When lines were thick
And colors the rage

Before the world
So black and white
Became.

1. Introduction

Why another book?

If my first book was all about prolonging childhood as long as possible, this book is about being a grownup. As one of my oldest, dearest friends has pointed out, at least in the Jewish tradition, only those over the age of fifty are allowed to dispense wisdom. I have certainly earned those wings! Ironic, of course that I'm taking lessons on Judaism from my fellow Catholic grade-school classmate, both of us raised in the outermost nearly-rural suburban satellites of Chicago. Nevertheless, dispense wisdom I shall.

In the first book, *Go Forward, Support! The Rugby of Life*, I included any number of quotes or statements to the effect that "too much is never enough," and "God protects drunks and children; try to remain both at all times." In truth, God protects neither, nor can He even protect us from ourselves. Take the City of New Orleans for example, which for years held fast to the comforting delusion that they were protected and that no major hurricane would ever strike their fair city. They would party and celebrate on Bourbon Street every time the hurricane warnings proved false and the storm veered off its course, missing the city. Until the time it didn't. It has been over ten years since Katrina, and some might ask, what are the odds of that happening again? Lightning doesn't strike twice. We should be safe for a while, right? When you think in geologic time scales, things happen across a much longer playing field. Simply put, if you wait long enough, the chance is 100 percent. There is an infinite difference between improbable and impossible.

There is a verse in the Bible (Matthew 10:29-31), that says something along the lines of, "If the Lord protecteth even the sparrow, certainly the Lord shall protect you." Or, more precisely:

> *Are not two sparrows sold for a penny? Yet not one of them will fall to the ground outside your Father's care. And even the hairs of your very head are all numbered. So, don't be afraid; you are worth more than many sparrows.*

One morning on my way to work, sitting at a stoplight, I saw something fall through the air, from atop the traffic light that hangs out over the center of the intersection. At first I thought it might have been snow, but then I realized to my horror that it was a living thing, as I caught a glimpse of its yellow beak. When the light turned green, as I drove past, I looked to the ground, and saw the wispy feathers, the frail lifeless body of the baby bird on the pavement. Some fool mother bird had built her nest on the traffic light.

Simple lesson: God couldn't protect or save that bird. Neither could I, and neither could its mother.

Mothers can't protect their children from everything, as much and as hard as they might try. And try, as grownups, we will. I can guarantee you, there was one night in America when practically every parent lied to their children as they put them to bed, and reassured them that everything was going to be alright, when in fact, we knew nothing of the sort. If anything, the only thing we knew for sure the night of September 11th was that nothing was going to be okay or the same again for a very long time, if ever again. War had come to us. That's just what we have to do sometimes as grownups. We lie.

Maybe even just by saying everything is going to be okay, it makes us feel like there is a better chance of its all being okay. I remember hearing General Colin L. Powell (U.S. Army, Ret.) at the 2015 Sage Summit, in conversation with CEO Stephen Kelly and Deepak Chopra, where he shared his first rule of leadership, when getting bad news: "It's not as bad as you think. It will be better in the morning. It's not a prediction, it's a hope." All thirteen rules are captured in his book, *It Worked for Me: In Life and Leadership* (Powell, 2012).

And sometimes we have to tell the hard truths that no one wants to hear. That's also part of being a grownup. Or, as President Truman once said: "I never did give anyone hell. I told them the truth, and they thought it was hell."

There are three reasons for this second book. In the first book, I wrote as a child, but now I write as a grownup, having gone through many transitions and weathered many storms: turning fifty, becoming a supervisor, and suffering so much loss. They have been the best of times and the worst of times. I've seen things I never wanted to see. I've been in impossible situations. Since the first book, I lost my sister – my sounding board, my social conscience, someone who could always tell me what needed to be done. And then I lost my mom, and I had no one to ask permission from anymore, and no one to take care of, and I knew I was really on my own, the grown-up.

I've also seen some of the happiest days of my life. We finally got married. After so much loss, we needed a joyful occasion.

I've seen things I never thought I would see. For example, same-sex marriage. In the first book, I talked about how the LGBTQ community might always stay on the fringe of mainstream society, like the Meccas on the coasts, Provincetown and San Francisco. I far underestimated the power of assimilation and acceptance as more people came out, and society adjusted and evolved. No longer completely foreign, LGBTQ people were seen increasingly to be everywhere, brothers, sisters, cousins, teachers, students, co-workers, neighbors. And the world kept spinning. My only fear now is that this evolution is not a continuous forward trek, but instead follows the arc of a swinging pendulum. All the forward progress we have made could be reversed and come unraveled so quickly, if the pendulum swings back. Tides change, empires rise and fall. "Little is a stone," to quote a line from the poem, "Burning the Old Year," by poet Naomi Shihab Nye. And even stones erode away.

The second reason I write again is that I feel like I have something more to say, different from what was in the first book. That's the writer's conceit, thinking that I might have something to say, that other people might want to hear. When my grandniece learned I had written a book, she surprised me by asking, "Why?" I thought everyone wanted to write a book, tell their story, and share it with the world. The urge to write springs from within: it's a primal need. The mind wanders, ponders, and seizes on a topic, then links it to another story or thought. Jotting it all down in one of my many notebooks, I sketch it out on paper before it flees, and then ultimately string this series of thoughts together in a logical order, making some sense of it all, weaving and stitching ideas together, sometimes looping back around, and building an overall coherent mosaic that – hopefully – tells a story. It's as satisfying as kneading and shaping a bread dough. It's both an itch and a need. What's inside needs to be put in order, and put out on paper.

Just like clams, who are also "filter feeders," dining on all the passing flotsam and jetsam, I too am happiest taking it all in, what's happening around me, catching bits and bytes of the daily news, reworking it and re-shaping it, ultimately putting it all back together into something new. Thus, the happy clam.

Lastly, I write again, because the first book sold so well. Just kidding! Given the number of boxes of books remaining in our laundry room, I can be pretty sure that most of you have not read it yet. Thus, I will be taking great liberty and shamelessly recycling and reusing material from it, and yet it will still seem nice and fresh and new to most of you!

2. Chasing Happiness

So, that's how this book started. I wanted to find ways for people (including myself) to be happier. There is an entire body of study devoted to the psychology of happiness, from the earliest works of William James, the founder of American psychology, to the recent works of Martin E. P. Seligman (author of *Learned Optimism*, and *What We Can Change*) and Matthew Gilbert (*Stumbling on Happiness*), there is no shortage of advice out there on finding this elusive state of happiness.

There are some key, fundamental findings, such as: optimists really do have more fun (Seligman, 1990); we are horrible predictors of what will make us happy; and we don't even know when we are truly happy even while it is happening (Gilbert, 2006). It seems to be best recognized either in retrospect, or in anticipation of a future event (such as looking forward to a vacation). Things in the past and in the future always look far better than they really were or will turn out to be. And things in the present always look bigger and worse than they really are.

This explains why happiness seems so elusive: it's always moving. You can see it ahead of you, and behind you, but you don't even realize it when you are right in the very midst of it.

In the first book, I quoted the line from the Joe Jackson song about needing to know what you want before you can get what you want, and it seemed true at the time, but I now realize it's only half true at best, given that we don't know what will make us happy, and can best recognize it only in retrospect, and meanwhile there are all the surprising, random, chance things that can bring ridiculous joy. If we limit ourselves to what we can imagine, we confine ourselves. There's a universe beyond what we can imagine.

Given people's inability to recognize happiness, even while soaking in it, or accurately predict what will make them happy, I always wish people "much happiness and success," rather than a particular outcome. Since I don't know specifically what will actually bring them happiness, and ironically, probably neither do they, I simply hope that the right things happen that will result in happiness for them, and if they have happiness, success will follow.

Happiness researchers have found that about 50 percent of our happiness is determined by nature (i.e., "what we're born with," as sort of a set point). So, yes, it's true, some people are literally just born happier than others. Another 40 percent is determined by what we do ("intentional activity"), and only 10 percent by our particular circumstances (Etcoff, 2015; Lyubomirsky, et al., 2005; Lyubomirsky, 2007). Happiness is viewed as being additive, as shown in this simple formula:

H = Nature + Actions + Circumstances

Measuring happiness is a little bit tricky, because it is subjective. Researchers have developed a number of instruments, tests, and surveys, to gauge an individual's happiness (Sugay, 2019).

I am not a researcher, but I believe it's the way that one looks at life's events, one's perspective, that will have a larger factor in calculating one's happiness. Rather than summing things up, I see perspective as being a multiplier:

H = P x (Life Events + People + Stuff)

If you want to increase your happiness, your energy would be best spent working on changing your perspective multiplier, rather than chasing things that we think will make us happy. Perspective is the far greater factor, because it allows you to see and value what you have in life, instead of feeling always empty and hungry for what you don't have. You can have a lot of stuff inside the parenthesis in the equation above, but if you lack perspective, you may not truly value or appreciate it. It's like multiplying a large number by zero. We could put a lot of effort into chasing these things, and still find we're not much happier, or as happy as we thought we would be. It also may be physically difficult – or impossible – to change much in the Life Events category, the hand we're dealt. If you have good perspective, you will be able to see and value all that you have in life, fostering gratitude, and feeling blessed, lucky, fortunate. Happiness may be less about the landscape you're looking at, and far more about the lens through which you view it, and what your mind's eye chooses to focus on. This brings to mind one of my favorite quotes by Oscar Wilde:

We are all lying in the gutter, but some of us are looking at the stars.

Is it possible to change one's focus? One's perspective? One's lens? Are these fixed? Or, are we malleable? Can one's mindset be gently nudged? And if so, how? Or, are we destined to be captive to our minds, our feelings, our natural reactions to life events? Are our emotional reflexes every bit as involuntary as our physical reflexes, and outside our control?

There is a growing body of research showing that happiness actually follows a fairly standard, predictable course over the span of one's lifetime, ultimately reaching its lowest point at about age fifty, and then increasing again after that (Bakalar, 2010; Blanchflower and Oswald, 2017; Ingraham, 2017;

Rauch, 2014; Stone, et al., 2010). Yes, ironically, the happiness curve plot is smile-shaped. Having somewhat recently passed this milestone myself, I can think of many good reasons why fifty might be the low point, but also three reasons for fifty's being a turning point.

Fifty is probably about the point that the burdens and responsibilities of being a grownup reach a maximum:

Growing children.

Aging parents.

Increased responsibility at work, caring about the careers of others and the future of the organization, and maybe the entire world, and the legacy left by your generation.

With great responsibility comes great stress. If fifty had a bumper sticker, it would say, "It's not about me."

After fifty, maybe it becomes easier to:

Care a little less.

Forget more.

Take nothing personally.

Early on in our lives and careers and families, every single little thing seems so critically important, as we try to carve out our place and make our path in the world. Caring is highly valued and rewarded. After a few laps around the track, you start to realize that a looser grip on the wheel can also work just as well, taking far less effort, stress, and energy. You still care, but you're bothered less by things. Setbacks are not the end of the world; they are just the next set of obstacles to be overcome. They're just the landscape. You realize that you don't have control over everything. Things that at first looked like a complete disaster turn out okay, while other things that seemed to be going along swimmingly suddenly implode without warning. Yet, there's something to be learned from every experience, and maybe in some crazy way, everything happens for a reason.

In my last book, I wrote a lot about the importance of forgiving, but in fact forgetting is almost equally as effective. I'm not talking about cognitive decline, and certainly not Alzheimer's or dementia, but simply having a larger universe of experiences against which these smaller slights and insults can play out, fading away and becoming nothing more than background noise, and no longer looming large. It's a matter of scale. You need big stuff to see how small the small stuff really is. And, of course, we all know we shouldn't sweat the small stuff (Carlson, 1997).

There is power in letting go. Emotion is like a muscle. We spend so much time building muscle, by lifting, pulling, and pushing, all to build and flex and hang on, but it actually takes just as much effort – and maybe more – to let go, to relax and release those muscles. We have to *not* care sometimes. Otherwise, we are all so unbelievably fragile, delicate, and breakable. We have to be strong enough to not get knocked down as we are buffeted by life's blows, and yet also know that others may be fragile, too.

Forgiveness helps us let go. As my dad says, "Forgiveness is the fastest way to get rid of anger." Study after study shows that hanging on to past hurts and indignities brings us down, and letting go is freeing (Lewis, 2015; Zheng, et al., 2015). There's a new book out by Katherine Schwarzenegger Pratt on precisely this topic, all about how forgiveness is a gift we give ourselves (Pratt, 2020).

Lastly, there is freedom in not taking anything personally. There are two possible explanations when you feel that someone has offended you. Either it wasn't meant that way, and you're getting upset and over-reacting over nothing, or it really *was* meant that way, in which case it may say more about the other person than it does about you. As the saying goes, don't let the bastards get you down. Walk tall and walk away when you need to. Don't be overly swayed by just one person's opinion, based solely on their narrow view of the world. Do try to see things through their eyes, and calmly and objectively look for any points that may have some validity and merit.

One of the most disarming things you can say to defuse a conflict is, "Maybe you're right; maybe I'm wrong." It opens the door to the possibility for both of you that one's reality may be malleable, multi-dimensional, and not immutable after all. Maintaining one's sense of dignity is essential, but so is considering the possibility that one has inadvertently stepped on someone else's feelings and sense of self worth. It's all rather delicate. We are all surprisingly fragile.

One of the most important lessons I learned from rugby is how to fall and get back up. Over and over again.

If we were to ask the question, "What is human life's chief concern?" one of the answers we should receive would be: "It is happiness." How to gain, how to keep, how to recover happiness, is in fact for most men at all times the secret motive of all they do, and of all they are willing to endure.

William James
Father of American Psychology
From the Gifford Lectures
Delivered at Edinburgh in 1901-1902

3. Choosing Happiness

The concept that we can control how happy we are seems revolutionary, but the idea has been contemplated by philosophers and psychologists alike since the dawn of humankind. Even in William James' time, there was a "mind-cure" movement, as he called it, made all the more poignant given that he himself suffered serious depression.

We've all heard it said, that we are "entitled to our feelings," and "can't help how we feel." The funny thing is, the more you hear this, the more you believe it. Feelings are seen as a reflex, as natural and uncontrollable a response as the jerk of the knee after a tap with the hammer. We feel things in response to external stimuli. To do otherwise would require deliberate, conscious thought, work, effort, and action.

Yet, who wouldn't want to be happier? What if someone told you there was a magic pill that could make you happier? Well, there are some out there, and there is a place for those, too. But, what if there was a natural way to get a little happier just by exerting some conscious, deliberate effort, changing the way you think, and altering your perspective? Can you change your mind about the way you feel?

There's a saying: "We are about as happy as we make our minds up to be." Source: the tag on a tea bag. I probably still have it somewhere. The tag, that is, not the bag. The quote might have been from Abraham Lincoln, but that has not been confirmed. Not that we should take all our life wisdom and advice from a tea bag, fortune cookie, or horoscope, but sometimes they're right!

The question becomes: Do you want to be happy? Happier, at least?

As the story goes, when John Lennon was young, he was asked what he wanted to be when he grew up. He answered: Happy. His teachers told him that he had not understood the question. He told them they didn't understand life. The veracity of this tale can't be substantiated, and it has been attributed to at least two other celebrities, including Goldie Hawn and Linus, the Peanuts character, except that Linus said, "Outrageously happy." We might also say that he's a dreamer, waiting in that pumpkin patch every year for the Great Pumpkin. Regardless, whether it was Linus, Goldie Hawn, or John Lennon, same difference, we have multiple iconic figures all sharing the same desire: to be happy.

There are several recent books on this topic. Daniel Gilbert's book, *Stumbling on Happiness*, reveals that we humans are exceptionally poor at predicting what will bring us happiness, or even knowing when we are happy in the present. Happiness is best perceived (and perhaps amplified) when looking back at it in the rearview mirror. So, when we are currently happy right now *and we know it* – well, that is indeed a feat worthy of clapping our hands!

There are also many studies and books showing all the benefits of being happy, such as *The Happiness Advantage: How a Positive Brain Fuels Success in Work and Life*, by Shawn Achor. We may have thought success brings happiness, but it turns out it's the other way around: happiness leads to success. There are many benefits to being happier, such as increased creativity and productivity, and he lays them all out in his book, along with advice on practices that can help get you there (Achor, 2010; Schulte, 2015).

In addition to all the obvious benefits of being happier – feeling good, safe, successful, secure, liked – there is the added bonus that the happier you are, the happier your network will be. Happiness is contagious, according to a study in the British Medical Journal (Fowler and Christakis, 2008; Johnson, 2008). Your friends', family's, and neighbors' happiness are all connected, and so the happier they are, the happier you will be, and vice versa. There is an astonishingly far-reaching ripple effect.

Unfortunately, stress is also contagious, through the smell of our sweat, between mothers and infants, as well as between strangers (de Groot, Smeets, and Semin, 2015; Mujica-Parodi, et al., 2009; Waters, West, and Mendes, 2014). It's not unique to humans, in fact it's something biochemical that's probably shared across the animal kingdom.

Even studies of voles — common field mice — find that a stressed vole will bring their stress home with them, and cause an uptick in stress hormones in their cage-mates (Burkett, et al., 2016; Hartnett, 2016). Perhaps most encouraging, the researchers also observed the other voles trying to comfort the stressed-out mouse. We're not all that different.

It seems that we are in the midst of multiple public health crises, with both stress and loneliness at epidemic levels. It's hard to be happy if you're stressed or lonely or both.

We have more ways to connect than ever before, thanks to cell phones and social media, and yet studies show that people feel just as lonely as ever before. There's a brand new book out all about loneliness, ironically titled *Together*, by Dr. Vivek H. Murthy. It was while serving as the 19th U.S. Surgeon General that he came to recognize loneliness as a growing public health crisis.

The insurance company, Cigna, sponsored a survey conducted by Ipsos in 2018, which found that almost half of Americans report sometimes or always feeling alone or left out, and feeling as though no one knows them well (Cigna and Ipsos, 2018). So, if you're feeling lonely, you're not alone. Studies have shown that loneliness has about the same effect on mortality as smoking 15 cigarettes per day (Holt-Lunstad, et al., 2015). The greatest predictor of poor health and loneliness was a lack of in-person interactions. Those who had frequent meaningful face-to-face interactions were least lonely, and loneliness was also found to decrease with age (Cigna and Ipsos, 2018; Bruce, et al., 2019).

Cigna conducted a follow-on survey in 2019 to look at loneliness in the workplace (Cigna, 2020). They surveyed over 10,000 U.S. adults, and found that the majority of those in Generation Z (79%) and Millennials (71%) are lonely, compared to half of Boomers (50%). Workplace culture, work-life balance, flexibility, communication, and quality of working relationships seemed to be the greatest factors affecting scores.

At the risk of sounding old, there was a time before cell phones and e-mail, when long distance phone calls were a special luxury, and people wrote letters. How often do we send a quick text or e-mail instead of calling or seeing someone in person? It takes energy to engage with people, but well worth the investment. Now, even when people get together, they're often on their phones. Conversation – and real human interaction – is becoming a lost art.

Similar to loneliness, stress brings with it a whole host of bad actors: elevated heart rate, high blood pressure, weakened immune system, weight gain (particularly unhealthy belly fat), and other negative health impacts (Epel, et al., 2000). To make matters worse, belly fat has been linked with an increased risk of developing dementia (Prior, 2020). Increased body fat and waist size have been correlated with shrinkage of the memory centers in the gray matter of the brain (Hamer and Batty, 2019).

Studies have also shown that stress can impact our ethics. In one study, people were more inclined to cheat when under greater stress, due to the combination of elevated levels of both cortisol and testosterone (Lee, et al., 2015; Shellenbarger, 2015; Weintraub, 2015).

Another study found that people who felt stressed were less likely to help a stranger they encountered along their way – and these were Divinity School students (Darley and Batson, 1973). In this experiment, whether or not people stopped to help the stranger had almost nothing to do with how virtuous they were, and everything to do with how late they were. This helps explain the stress created by our daily commute. It's eye-opening to realize how much of our behavior is situational, condition-dependent, and so heavily influenced by exterior factors in the environment around us. Stress hinders our ability to be our best versions of ourselves, as people are wont to say these days.

Not all stress is bad. Sometimes we need those fight-or-flee brain chemicals as a matter of survival. Stress can be helpful sometimes, such as when we're gearing up for the big game, or taking on new challenges. It's just unhealthy to live in that zone all the time.

Even bad stress, traumatic stress, has the potential to lead to post-traumatic growth, like new life springing forth after a forest fire (Hayward, 2013; Rendon, 2015). Recovery from such deep 'soul injuries' is difficult, but possible, some say, through self compassion and reconnecting with people (Grassman 2015; van der Kolk, 2014).

One of the most important people we can forgive might be ourselves. Studies show that practicing self-compassion and self-forgiveness can provide the impetus for making positive change (Breines and Chen, 2012; Lewis, 2012). After all, how can we forgive others, if we're unable to forgive ourselves? As I always say, there is something to be learned from every experience, no matter how painful.

That which hurts, also instructs.

Benjamin Franklin

So, let's say you agree with these premises and decide that you would like to be happier. How does that sort of change happen? Do you want to change? As the old joke goes:

Q: How many psychiatrists does it take to change a light bulb?

A: It doesn't matter how many there are. The light bulb has to want to change.

Another recent book, *The Power of Habit*, by Charles Duhigg, argues that life is simply a series of habits, and it is simply by making better, conscious choices that we can develop the right habits that will lead to greater happiness.

Life can be repetitious, and so maybe changing up our routine is just what we need to pull ourselves out of a rut. (Makes sense, given that the two words, rut and routine, share a common word origin, from the French.) Sometimes, when days follow days, one after another, people reference the movie, *Groundhog Day*, when Bill Murray's character keeps waking up and re-living the same day over and over again. Until he gets it right. (Spoiler Alert.) He finally starts paying attention to the other people in his day, and when he learns that his love interest, Andie MacDowell, enjoys piano, he even starts taking piano lessons. He uses every day to better himself, to woo Andie, despite his complete loss of control to change his time and place in the world. The only thing he can change is himself.

So, how does change happen? Bit by bit. One day at a time. Which brings me to another one of my favorite movies: *Shawshank Redemption*. (Spoiler Alert) Trapped in prison, the main character finds a way to dig his way out, one pocket full of dirt at a time. In a way, I had my own personal *Shawshank Redemption* in my first book, writing my way out, as a release from my day job, one page at a time. All the while, I was a good employee, worked hard, very hard, and then one day I became supervisor, and the world changed, and yet it also didn't. I thought I'd really be able to make a difference and change things. Of course, I had to learn the hard lesson all over again that I still couldn't change other people. The only person I could change was myself, and that would be hard enough.

How does this change get started? How does a body at rest break free of inertia and become a body in motion? It's like the moment a ball is put into play, whether a tennis serve, a baseball pitch, teeing off in golf, or a rugby scrum or lineout. What does it take? Making contact. What's the impetus? Do we need a wake-up call? I did.

I had been a supervisor for about three years. And, the first three years of being a supervisor coincided with the last three years of my sister's life. It was just a few months after Angie had passed away, and I was not sleeping well, the usual, waking in tears at three or four in the morning, and on top of this, there was still all the stress of work.

There was one night in particular, another night of restless sleep, not really sleeping at all, my mind racing through all the stresses in my life, mostly work, how would I rein in my 12-hour work days, and when would I have time left for me, and my love, and my life's creative pursuits, and how would I ever make these changes happen? And then I heard a voice. In my dream? But, I was thinking, so I couldn't have been dreaming, right? And the voice said: "Do you *want* to change?"

This was a new question.

To some degree, I had to accept and own it, that I was ultimately choosing all my actions, choosing to stay late, choosing to miss dinner and work until 8:00 at night, choosing not to have time for my love, choosing not to exercise. And by choosing to do all of these things, I was expressing through my actions what I wanted to do. I had to own it, that even though I didn't exactly love my current life situation, I was doing exactly what I chose to do.

I had to ask myself the hard question: Did I really want to change? And if so, then how?

4. Your Happy Place

The best place to start is with simple, easy things. Little things. We are unbelievably impressionable, susceptible, prone to the lightest of suggestion, easily influenced by the most subtle or subliminal messages, as they reach into our subconscious river of thought. It turns out we are psychologically like the color-changing chameleon, or the quivering jellyfish, simply taking on the color and ambiance of the waters in which we swim. You can fight it and deny it, or accept it and take advantage of it, just as an Olympic athlete picks a slightly more aerodynamic sled or fabric to gain a competitive edge, an advantage. Same here, and pick wisely, for what you wish for may come true.

To quote Psalm 23: "Surely goodness and mercy shall follow me all the days of my life." Maybe instead we should be the ones following and pursuing goodness and mercy.

But let us start with the small things. While the world loves the chaos and excitement and drama of cataclysmic change, the blockbusters, the next big thing, there is an entire body of study devoted to the cumulative effect of a lot of little changes, the power of incremental change. In geology, the history of our planet has been shaped by a mix of catastrophic change (meteor impacts, volcanic eruptions, earthquakes, floods, extinctions) and gradual, uniform processes playing out slowly over thousands and millions of years (erosion, sedimentation, evolution of life). So, too are our lives. *Normal* is but the stage on which all our life's dramas are played out upon.

Business books spend a lot of time on the power of big, bold, new ideas, but at least one book also acknowledges the power of simply creating an environment in which suggestions can flourish: *Ideas Are Free*, by Alan G. Robinson and Dean M. Schroeder. By creating the right environment, where suggestions are encouraged, the whole organization benefits by having people who are more engaged, and constantly thinking of ways to make things better. While most of the ideas may result in small changes, the environment is ripe for coming up with big ideas too.

It makes sense to start with what is do-able. "You have to meet people where they are," as my sister always said. Numerous studies also support the power of small, incremental change, from making your bed every morning (McRaven, 2017), to paying bills and saving money (Brown and Lahey, 2014). The path to big wins is paved with small victories, though

I have to confess, I don't always make my bed. Time is too precious in my book.

There are a lot of little things we can do to change our surroundings, and put ourselves in a happier frame of mind: colors, smells, plants, pets, and music, to name a few.

The home improvement stores have it right; a bucket of paint can change a room. There are many schools of thought on the meaning and influence of colors, from scientific studies to chakras to Feng Shui. They all seem to agree at least on the effects of the following colors.

Greens are calming and spa-like. Thus, the 'green rooms' where performers go to relax before going on stage. Green is the color of grass, leaves, plants, and trees. It's the color of life itself. Green has been called the color of hope.

Yellows are bright and happy. Reds add excitement, but a little goes a long way. Blues are peaceful, but from a home design standpoint, terribly difficult to match and coordinate with, which can create added stress. There are so many shades of blue. Browns are genuine, earthy, and grounding. Black and white are serious. The best advice is to add some green and yellow to your surroundings where you can, and bring some nature inside.

Colors, in general, are more interesting than beige. They can call it "biscuit," but it's still beige. I am still waiting for the sequel to *Fifty Shades of Gray*, when they have been married a while, and are spending a day sorting through paint chips at the local Home Depot. It would be called *Fifty Shades of Beige*. With that said, out with the beige, and in with some color!

Plants can also contribute to a happier and more peaceful environment. It helps that they're green. They are also pretty good air cleaners, taking in carbon dioxide, and exhaling oxygen during the day through the magic of photosynthesis. Some studies even show that some plants might help remove harmful household chemicals from the air. Oxygen is good. Living things are good.

Multiple studies show that plants in the workplace can both increase productivity (Niewenhuis, et al., 2014; University of Exeter, 2014), and reduce stress levels (Toyoda, et al., 2019). Even by doing something as simple as gazing at a small plant three minutes each day, people experienced a decrease in heart rate and felt less stressed afterwards.

Studies have also found that interacting with nature can benefit individuals suffering from depression (Berman, et al., 2012). A simple walk through a natural setting improved mood and increased memory span, serving almost like a reset button. Re-connecting with nature seems to hit a primal need within us, sometimes lost in the work-a-day world.

Surprisingly, even fake plants can have almost the same positive effect on mood, and require a lot less care, aside from the occasional dusting. We found some very realistic looking plants and flowers to spruce up my mom's room when she was in the nursing home. There was this wooden herb box of basil, sage, and rosemary that looked so real, right down to the fake soil, that I'm pretty sure more than once they got watered. We also found some bright, cheery faux Gerbera daisies always blooming in a glass vase. And doesn't faux sound so much better than fake?

I didn't know it at the time but it turns out that there are multiple studies demonstrating the benefits of plants (real or fake) on patients' recovery in the hospital (Beukeboom, Langeveld, and Tanja-Dijkstra, 2012; Fulton, 2014; Park and Mattson, 2008, 2009; Ulrich, 1984). Patients with plants in their room (foliage or flowering) experienced faster, smoother recoveries, were less stressed, and required less pain medication. Even just having a view of nature out the window was found to have a positive effect on patient recovery (Ulrich, 1984). So, our natural instinct to bring flowers when someone is sick or feeling down is spot on. It's nice that the science also supports it.

Some of this stuff is as simple as the song from *The Sound of Music*, simply surrounding yourself with some of your favorite things, including whiskers on kittens, even when they're tickling your nose to wake you up at three or four in the morning! Pets, and petting your pets, have been shown to reduce heart rate and lower blood pressure – except when you're yelling at them for chewing your plants.

It all has to do with brain biochemistry. Interacting with pets releases neurotransmitters like oxytocin, endorphins, dopamine, and serotonin, that all give you that feel-good feeling (Montgomery, 2015; Olmert, 2009). There is the companionship and unconditional love, the bond that transcends words. As the bumper sticker says, "Who rescued who?"

Even pets you can't pet can have a positive effect. It has been scientifically shown that just *watching* fish can also lower your heart rate and decrease blood pressure (Cracknell, et al., 2015; Knapton, 2015). With no harmful side effects! Well, aside from the fact that fish might smell a little, well, fishy.

Aromatherapy is yet another way to manipulate your environment to modify your mood, and overcome that fishy smell of the new aquarium you just purchased. Citrus is said to be cheering: lemon, bergamot, and yuzu, to name just a few.

Smells have some of the deepest, strongest roots in memory. Just by smelling certain scents, you can conjure up happy memories: wood smoke, campfires, pine needles, Christmas trees and cookies, lilacs on Mother's Day, bread baking, roast beef on a Sunday afternoon, fresh mown grass, and spring-time mud. While the easiest way to generate these smells might be by lighting a scented candle, the best way is to actually have a real wood fire, and bake some real cookies.

Favorite foods – in moderation – can also take you to a happier place. Yes, a Happy Meal can still make me happy. More on this later.

Music is another tool to set the tone, create ambience, and lift your mood. If you want to be happier, listen to more upbeat music. Just think of Snoopy, in *It's the Great Pumpkin, Charlie Brown*, when he listens and reacts to the music Schroeder is playing on the piano, causing him to dance exuberantly, then sob inconsolably as the mood of the song changes. We are just like that. It's for that same reason that armies have rousing marching songs, movies have soundtracks, sports teams have marching bands, and stadiums have DJs. It's no accident that the New England Patriots football team plays "Crazy Train," by Ozzy Osbourne, at the start of each home game, and "Sweet Caroline" plays at the seventh inning stretch of Red Sox games at Fenway. Music can get people pumped up, and create a common heartbeat within a crowd.

We often gravitate towards certain music genres and bands, based on how we're feeling. The problem is that someone who's feeling down will gravitate toward sad or downbeat music, to match their mood, further reinforcing it (Lewis, 2015; Millgram, et al., 2015). It might take a little work, but if you're feeling down, you'd be better off seeking out happier, more upbeat music, to help lift you out of that rut. Try instead literally changing the channel. Try out a totally different station or genre. If you've never listened to country or classical music, give it a shot. Try something different.

In the same way, just as you can change what you're hearing, you can also change what you're seeing, by changing what you're putting in front of your eyes to see. For example, put up a couple of pictures that speak to you. Abstract, realistic, surrealistic, classical, or modern. If you can't find or afford originals, then department store prints and posters will work just as well. I remember in college decorating my dorm room with free travel posters. Or create your own. It needn't be perfect; it need only be yours.

Another study shows the surprising effect that gazing at a painting can have (Kotz, 2013; Roberts, 2013). Professor Jennifer Roberts at Harvard University has her students gaze at an original painting for three hours, to gain an appreciation for the depth of detail in the work.

Similar resets can be accomplished in a variety of other ways, through the practice of mindfulness, or just taking time out to re-direct our gaze and re-direct our mind by doing something different, whether it's looking at art, enjoying nature, or just going for a walk (Oppezzo and Schwartz, 2014; Seppälä, 2016). We need silence and downtime as much as we need all the other "productive" parts of our lives.

Many people struggle with the idea of quiet time, and shutting out the distractions of the world. In one study, a surprising number of participants, when faced with spending time alone with their thoughts, elected to give themselves a brief electrical shock (Johnson, 2014; Wilson, et al., 2014). Pain was preferable to boredom.

Much has been written about the effect that technology is having on our brains, both shrinking our attention span and destroying our ability to concentrate and focus. It began with e-mail ("You've got mail!"), and grew with the texts and social media that followed. Each time we hear that notification, we're like Pavlov's dogs, drooling and barking at it. We're wired for immediate gratification, and each time we open something, our brain releases more of those feel-good chemicals. Every time we do this, we're distracting ourselves from the task at hand, and the people right in front of us. The more we do it, the more we want to do it, and the greater effect it can have on our brains.

We now know there is something called "neuroplasticity," and brains can change over time, depending on how we use them. There is a classic study that demonstrated this by doing MRI's on London taxi and bus drivers (Maguire, Woollett, and Spiers, 2006). The study found that the part of the brain that processes spatial intelligence, in the mid-posterior hippocampus, was much larger in taxi drivers, and size was correlated with the number of years of experience navigating the complex traffic network of London. The more this part of the brain was used, the more it grew. This growth was accompanied by a reduction elsewhere, in the anterior hippocampus, resulting in a reduced ability to create new spatial memories.

In our case, our electronic media interaction comes at the expense of our social interactions. Our connectedness to everything leaves us less able to concentrate on one thing, leaving us feeling mentally scattered; literally "scatter-brained." (Ironically, I couldn't settle on a single reference to cite here, as there were simply too many to choose from!)

Thus, there is something to be said for having a sense of order in one's life, as well as in one's mind. If everything is in disarray, start with just one corner of the room. When I bought my first little condo many years ago, it had been in foreclosure and was in rough shape. I remember cleaning off just one small corner of the Formica countertop, and seeing the bright surface underneath, feeling hope that it could be made whole again. It is a blessing, to make your home a sanctuary, a safe and peaceful place away from the noise of the world.

In yoga, one of the tenets of good living (Niyamas) is called Saucha, which is usually described as purity and cleanliness, but can also be more broadly read as orderliness. One of the yoga instructors I had was an Army veteran, and she described how, going into a battlefield environment, where anything can happen, maintaining Saucha, by keeping her field kit organized, was a way to exert some control over one part of her environment, when so much of everything else in her world was subject to sudden change and out of her control. This order in one corner of her world was a way to give herself some small sense of peace and calm.

There is of course the much larger practice of Feng Shui, which promotes harmonious settings by considering nature and energy flow in their design. It's rooted in a mix of spiritual beliefs, superstition, and common sense design practices. For example, sharp edges are to be avoided, because they can focus and re-direct bad energy - 'bad Qi' - at you (Sertori, 1998). I don't know how true this is, but I can say for sure that when I hit my elbow on the sharp edges of our dining room chairs, it's definitely painful. If you believe in it, then it probably works for you. Even if you don't believe in it, there are things that are worth thinking about, as far as colors, lighting, and landscape, and how and where you build your home, such as ensuring optimal exposure to the sun, and avoiding floodplains (Hermes, 2002).

Everything in this chapter really speaks to the practice of mindfulness; paying attention to what your mind pays attention to. This is not a new topic. The first book I read about it was literally titled *Mindfulness*, by Ellen Langer, published in 1989. And before that, came Dr. Herbert Benson's book, *The Relaxation Response*, in 1975, promoting meditation as a way to reduce stress and lower blood pressure. In ways, they were both ahead of their time. These subjects are made all the more relevant now by the levels of stress and distraction in society today.

If you don't have three hours to gaze at a painting, then gaze at a potted plant for three minutes. If you don't have a plant or even three minutes, then just take a deep breath. It will slow your heart rate and give you a greater sense of calm.

Inhale – count to three.
Hold for three.
Exhale – count to four.

Remember the old saying, if you're upset, count to ten? Well, add it up.

5. Happiness Is As Happiness Does

Even just thinking about all of this probably helps, by providing at a minimum, the benefit of the placebo effect. It was recently revealed that even the New England Patriots quarterback, Tom Brady, is on board, taking advice from his wife, Gisele Bündchen, carrying lucky stones for healing and protection, and saying mantras (Brown, 2019). Gisele is all about the "power of intention." Six Super Bowl wins later, who's going to argue with that?

Here's the funny thing. Being superstitious, and believing in good luck, can have a positive effect on actual outcomes, basically becoming a self-fulfilling prophecy (Damisch, Stoberock, and Mussweiler, 2010). During multiple experiments, performance on various physical and mental activities was enhanced when subjects invoked a lucky saying or lucky charm, which triggered an uptick in self-confidence, and an enhanced belief in their abilities.

In a similar way, taking on a "power pose" and making oneself large might trick the brain into feeling more confident, as researched and popularized by Harvard psychologist Amy Cuddy (Cuddy, 2015;

Cuddy, Schultz, and Fosse, 2018; Elsesser, 2018). Certainly, powerful people often seem to take up more space, and it appears likewise that the reverse is true, too. If we expand ourselves, in a powerful posture, our brains respond by making us feel more powerful and confident.

So much of life is about self-confidence, so anything we can do to build it provides a psychological advantage, which can translate into real, tangible, concrete results. Much has been written about the confidence gap between men and women (Clark, 2014; Kay and Shipman, 2014; Schmidt, 2015). For example, there was the study that found that women are far less likely than men to apply for a job unless they already met most of the qualification requirements, while men went in with the mindset that almost everything could be learned on the job (Hannon, 2014; Mohr, 2014). There is a cautionary tale in the number of studies showing the hazards of having too much confidence. Heightened testosterone levels were correlated with increased confidence, reduced reasoning skills, and impaired judgment (Huston, 2017). Still, confidence propels us to go forward, take risks, win, lose, learn, and grow.

What you *think* you can do might be even more important than what you *know* you can do.

Simply believing in the possibility of change confers a powerful and beneficial effect. In another study, when high school students were primed to believe that personality was malleable over time, and not fixed, they performed better in school (Lewis, 2014; Yeager, et al., 2014). Believing in the possibility of change probably triggered greater optimism, which also would have contributed to their success.

Studies have also shown that personally meaningful affirmations can help promote positive changes in behavior (Falk, et al., 2015; Kotz, 2015). What seemed to make the difference was tailoring the message to align with individuals' values.

Positive words or slogans, or mantras if you will, can have a subliminal effect on your attitude, but be careful of word choice. Studies have found that even the nature of the words used when delivering a message can have a subconscious effect on how one experiences the message (Newberg and Waldman, 2012). For example, the statement, "No problem," is meant to be positive, except that it in fact contains two negative words: "no" and "problem." Even though the intent is good, there is a subliminal bruising effect due to word choice. Instead of "no problem," try saying something like, "all good" or "happy to help."

Negative words (no, heavy, rain, illness, death, etc.) trip the ancient parts of the brain (amygdala, thalamus) that worry about and respond to threats (Talarovicova, et al., 2007). Positive words and thoughts feed the frontal lobe, in charge of executive function, thought, decision-making and emotional expression, representing the most-recently evolved part of the brain.

Even the sound of words can have a positive or negative effect. Studies show that "ee" words elicit positive, upbeat responses, while "oh" sounds result in negative reactions (Lewis, 2014; Rummer, et al., 2014). No wonder Homer Simpson is always saying "D'oh!" when things go wrong. It's the difference between "whee" and "woe." Think about it; when you say "ee" your mouth almost forms a smile. When you say "oh," it's the same sound and mouth shape we make when we're moaning.

The French enjoy a double benefit with the word, "oui," having both a positive sound and a positive meaning. We can also thank the French language for other laid-back words like "nonchalance," "laissez-faire," and "c'est la vie." So it goes; that's life. I don't know what it is, but the French certainly have a certain "je ne sais quoi."

"Que sera, sera" means the same thing in multiple languages (Spanish, Italian, and French, Spanish): What will be, will be.

Our sense of touch also plays a role in how we experience the world and how we feel emotionally (Ackerman, et al., 2010; Yong, 2010). Holding a smooth object can help make us feel more reassured, literally helping things to go more smoothly (Lewis, 2014; van Horen and Mussweiler, 2014). Rough, harsh, heavy objects will promote harshness, rigidity, and seriousness. So, think twice and choose wisely between the soft fleece or cotton jersey and the scratchy linen jacket.

There was a study that showed having a warm beverage when you meet someone may give you a slightly more favorable impression of them (Williams and Bargh, 2008), but the results have not been reproduced by other researchers, so the jury is still out on this one (Chabris, et al., 2019). Of course, psychology aside, it's always good hospitality to offer beverages to your guests.

Chewing gum has been shown to improve memory, heighten alertness, and enhance overall productivity (Allen and Smith, 2015; Scholey, 2014). And to think, we only got demerits in high school when we got caught chewing gum.

The smell of mint can also help you to better focus (Raudenbush, et al., 2009; Warm, Dember, and Parasuraman, 1991). Now, imagine the combined power of chewing minty gum! That's a slam dunk.

Too alert? Go find some lavender for its calming effect (Harada, et al., 2018).

The list goes on and on. There is a whole host of little things we can do, little actions that will move the needle just a tick, and help us be more productive and creative (Karlesky and Isbister, 2014; Shellenbarger, 2015; Wahl 2013). From playing with Play-Doh to clicking your pen, what appear to be only annoying or nervous fidgety habits can help us think more creatively and focus. These low-level distractions can actually help our brains to more fully focus on the problem at hand (Hullinger, 2015; Rotz and Wright, 2005). Injecting some playfulness, some fun, into our workday routine can also be just the thing to get us out of a rut and jump start some creativity (Seppälä, 2016).

Playing music in the background can not only cover up the sounds of other people's gum-chewing and pen-clicking around you, but can also boost productivity, spur creativity, and improve reading comprehension and retention (Burkus, 2017; Laverty, Edelstein, and Brink, 2016; Lesiuk, 2005; Mehta, Zhu, and Cheema, 2012). It has to be at just the right volume, not too loud, not too soft. I know some people swear by having absolute silence, but the theory is that some low-grade noise in the background forces the brain to work harder and focus more on taking in information, digesting and processing it, to overcome the slight distraction.

Even better, get a good night's sleep after reading something, and the brain will re-process and store the new information overnight. You will wake up with a better grasp of the material the next morning than you had right after reading it the night before. There are numerous studies supporting the finding that our brains pull a double duty, processing memories over the night shift (Rasch and Born, 2013; Schönauer, et al., 2017; Walker and Stickgold, 2006).

What if I told you there was one thing you could do to feel better every single day, and it's free, painless, legal, effortless, and requires no special equipment or skills? Sign me up, right? It sounds like a miracle, and it is simply this: get an extra hour of sleep each night. Most Americans are in a chronic state of sleep-deprivation. It is absolutely the simplest thing you can do, and it is almost entirely within your control. It's a habit worth pursuing and there has been a whole sleep enhancement industry that has sprung up around helping us do just this (Teitell, 2018). The difference one hour can make is highlighted by the statistics showing the spike in traffic accidents the day after we move our clocks forward in the spring for Daylight Savings Time (Downing, 2005; Weintraub, 2014). Certainly, getting one less hour of sleep than usual is detrimental to our health and well-being. Making sleep a priority might leave less time for other activities, but your increased effectiveness and improved mood will more than make up for it.

I remember hearing some advice that U.S. Army Lieutenant General Todd T. Semonite shared with his staff several years ago while speaking at a town hall meeting. He was the Commander of the North Atlantic Division of the U.S. Army Corps of Engineers at the time. He told the crowd, "There's only one thing you have to do here each day."

I thought this was great news, as my to-do lists are legendary. I truly believe if I put something on my list, it will eventually get done. I come from a long line of list-makers. So, this was exciting news, that I might be able to replace my entire to-do list with this one thing.

"This one thing," he said, "is this: Come in prepared to do your best." I thought that was pretty good advice.

I think an extra hour of sleep, and a good night's rest overall, will certainly help us all do our best each day. Not only will we be more productive and effective at work, but we'll probably also gain a bit in the happiness department.

I have a theory that the entire East Coast is one hour of sleep less happy and rested than the Midwest, and this could help explain why people in the Midwest are generally more open and friendly by nature. I remember my first day in Boston; I made the mistake of talking to people in the elevator. It's just not done here. People are just too frazzled, between the stress of long, aggravating commutes, and other demands on their time, they don't have the energy to engage in idle chit chat with a complete stranger.

Think about what an extra hour of sleep could do for people on the East Coast. Everyone wants to stay up and watch the news, see who wins the football or baseball game, how the movie ends, who won the Oscars, etc. To watch it happen in real time, people on the East Coast have to stay up an extra hour later than Midwesterners do, and yet there is still the same expectation at offices everywhere to open at 8:00 AM in both places. Of course Midwesterners are happier and friendlier; they're getting an extra hour of sleep every night compared to their East Coast counterparts.

I believe it would be in our nation's best interest to adjust the TV schedules up by an hour. Give us the news at 9:00, not 10:00, late night talk shows at 10:00, and bed by 11:00 at the latest, not midnight. Or they could re-run the late night talk shows at 5:00 or 6:00 in the morning. And no late-night football kick-offs, 7 PM at the latest. Yes, I know, folks on the West Coast might have to leave work early, but I don't think they'd mind that much.

The other alternative is to move permanently to the Atlantic Time Zone. Spring forward one hour and never look back (Emswiler, 2014).

Imagine all the people on the East Coast an extra hour more well-rested, happier, and that much more productive at work. Think of the possibilities – reduced traffic accidents, less road rage, fewer accidents and injuries at work. Think of what an effect this could have on business and the economy, given that the East Coast encompasses one of the most populated time zones.

Or, imagine what would happen if we switched to a four-day work week and how much stress that could alleviate. What would you do with that extra day? Imagine the savings, both in time and fuel, due to one less day of commuting. People could work four 10-hour days or four 9-hour days, and forego four hours of pay.

A case could even be made for the 6-hour work day (Glaveski, 2018). Sweden tried it, but found it too expensive, despite the positive benefits to the workers

(Kelly, 2020). Neighboring Finland also aspires to moving to a four-day work week someday.

A few companies, such as Shake Shack in the U.S., Microsoft in Japan, and Perpetual Guardian in New Zealand, have experimented with the four-day work week (Noguchi, 2020). Even with no reduction in salary, they have found productivity to be the same or better, accompanied by increased engagement (Noguchi, 2020; Perpetual Guardian, 2019). High levels of employee engagement and mutual trust with management are critical for it to succeed and make up for the lost hours.

Andrew Barnes, the CEO at Perpetual Guardian, an investment firm in New Zealand, decided to test out the four-day work week, out of a concern for the toll that working long hours was taking on the health of his people (Noguchi, 2020). He also reduced the number of meetings and eliminated open floor plans, to help facilitate focused efforts (Noguchi, 2020; Perpetual Guardian, 2019). People are getting the same amount of work done in four days, just by making better use of their time. Some also described how the extra day gives their brain a chance to rest and problem-solve (Noguchi, 2020). We all know the feeling of having that "Aha!" moment in the shower when we've allowed the subconscious brain to noodle on things a bit.

Other studies have also repeatedly demonstrated that working more hours does not necessarily translate into increased productivity, but instead diminishes overall effectiveness (Carmichael, 2015; Hoile, 2019; Pencavel, 2014). A 2014 study showed that when working anything beyond 50 hours, productivity plummets due to worker fatigue and stress (Pencavel, 2014). This truly is a case of where more is worse and less would be better. But we are all so keyed into the hourly pay paradigm.

Which would we rather have, more time or more money? We've all heard that money can't buy happiness. Not having enough money to make ends meet is stressful, but once earnings reach a certain point, studies show that more money does not necessarily translate into greater happiness (Jebb, et al., 2018). More on this later.

As my dad always says, "Once you have food, clothing, and shelter, everything else is a luxury. I'm glad I was born during the Depression; otherwise I wouldn't know how rich I am now."

Our culture glorifies shopping, buying, and spending; it's fun. There's the thrill of the hunt, plus it gives the brain a burst of immediate gratification. The problem is that the more we have, the more we want, it seems. We like stuff, but stuff does not promote long-term happiness, plus it's hard to feel happy or secure if you're carrying too much debt.

Since the advent of widespread credit card use in the 1980's, personal debt mushroomed, and the federal deficit essentially mirrored this trend over time. The only good news is that low interest rates limit the cost of credit, although they probably also serve to further enable people in their spending habits, to borrow and spend more. It's like saying that at least the crack cocaine is very affordable.

And yet, spending is critical to the economy. A shocking 70 percent of the U.S. economy is fueled by everyday consumer spending.

I wish we could find a way to make paying down debt and saving money just as exciting as shopping somehow. People like Suze Orman have tried to promote fiscal responsibility. What works best is to chip away at credit card balances, and pay off the one with the lowest balance first, as it provides a psychological sense of victory, making it more likely you'll keep it up (Lahey and Brown, 2014).

Here's a little more financial advice from Dad:

Don't be a slave to the lender.

Don't live for the love of money, but for what it can do for you.

Save some, spend some, and use some to help others.

How many U-Hauls can you pull behind your hearse?

The Local Purity World

Monday night is hell
At the local Purity world;
All those shoppers
With their shopping baskets full.

All our wants
All our needs
That they could all be filled
From some well-stocked shelf
At the Purity world Supreme!

Note: Purity Supreme was a local grocery store chain
in the Boston area, but was bought out and replaced
by Stop & Shop in 1995.

6. Healthy, Wealthy, and Wise

Benjamin Franklin probably didn't have to worry about missing any late-night television when he quipped his famous advice, "Early to bed, early to rise, makes a man healthy, wealthy, and wise." Being healthy and feeling good can certainly contribute to feeling happier. There are a lot of things we all know we should be doing to be healthy. Or healthier. They're all more easily said than done. The most basic advice: Eat right and exercise. We'll take those one at a time.

We all know we should eat lots of fruits and vegetables. Fish is good for us, but it's hard to eat it as frequently as we should, and so maybe fish oil supplements help. Those of us who live in a northern climate or work too much indoors, or both, don't get enough sunshine, and so maybe we should take some Vitamin D.

And yet, we are repeatedly told that our bodies best absorb and utilize nutrients from natural food sources, and not pills. What's a girl to do? Here are a few ideas.

Smoothies. We often start the day drinking a salad of greens (spinach, kale, romaine, parsley, or whatever is in season) with fruit (apples, bananas, pears, pineapple, mango, kiwi, orange, strawberries, blueberries), yogurt, milk, and various other items – ginger, chia seeds, etc. Who knew, all those years we were making chia pets with them, and now we find out that we should have been eating them all along. While this helps with eating more fresh fruits and vegetables, it hasn't helped with getting more fish. I worry that it's just a matter of time before fish wind up in the blender, too!

Sardines. Better than a fish oil supplement, and also a generous source of calcium and magnesium, the canned whole fillets (minus the head, please) offer a nutrient-packed meal. With a splash of lemon juice and hot chili sesame oil, served on a Triscuit, it's not as bad as you might think. And, given their small body size and shorter lifespan, they haven't had time to accumulate much mercury in their systems, unlike big fish, such as tuna.

Supplements. Speaking of magnesium and calcium, there is a world of nutritional supplements marketed, and while it's currently the Wild West, relatively unregulated, they are also unfortunately not well-integrated into mainstream medicine yet. There are few that have gone through the rigorous testing required (blind trials) to demonstrate efficacy. There are many out there that profess to promote health and happiness – rhodiola, CoQ10, etc. – but few with any documented studies to support the statements.

Magnesium has been shown to help against migraine (Maizels, et al., 2004; Peikert, et al., 1996.). The American Migraine Foundation suggests a dose of about 400 mg per day to help prevent migraines, which is just the USRDA for it, and so this is not an excessive dosage, but it is always best to start gradually. Always consult with your physician prior to using any supplements due to the potential for unintended side effects, contra-indications, and interactions with other medications. Any time you introduce anything new to your diet, start at a low dose and go slow. Low and slow. Every body reacts differently, and there could be as-yet unknown allergies and reactions.

Not only might magnesium help prevent migraines, it can also have a calming effect, promote better sleep, and possibly help treat depression (Abbasi, et al., 2012; Boyle, Lawton, and Dye, 2017; Tarleton, et al., 2017). Furthermore, stress depletes our bodies of magnesium (Cuciureanu and Vink, 2011). Even if you don't get migraines, you might want to check out magnesium. So much is written about calcium, but magnesium deserves equal attention. There is a yin-yang between them, as calcium works in the contraction of muscles, while magnesium allows them to relax. We focus so much on tightening our muscles, and holding on to things, both physically and mentally/emotionally, yet it is just as important to be able to release and let go of things. Some of the best sources of magnesium in food are pumpkin seeds and nuts, such as almonds, and cashews.

Tree nuts. The results are in, and people who eat nuts regularly are on average healthier (Bao, et al., 2013). In this seminal work, people who ate a serving of nuts daily weighed less and had a 20 percent lower death rate over the thirty-year period of the study, including a 29 percent reduction in death from heart disease, and 11 percent reduction for cancer. It only takes 1 ounce per day, which is equal to about a quarter cup; that's about 24 almonds, or 18 cashews, or 15 pecan halves. Or, say 20 mixed nuts total. They are easy to measure out with a ¼-cup measuring cup, and affordable when bought in bulk, and cheaper than most vitamins and supplements, plus they offer a nice helping of protein and fiber. The most affordable healthcare is the one you never have to use. As Hippocrates said, "Let food be thy medicine, and medicine thy food."

Exercise. Simply put, moving is good for you. We have all heard about how running releases endorphins, a natural happiness-inducing hormone. Even if you can't run, walk. It's easier on your joints anyway, and can serve as a quick reset during the day, increasing blood supply to the brain, and providing a fresh perspective when you return to the task at hand (Oppezzo and Schwartz, 2014). Better yet, add a companion and some nature and you get double bonus points (Berman, et al., 2012; Pinker, 2014, 2015).

One need not be an Olympic athlete to enjoy a moderate level of physical fitness. Whereas Olympians are sometimes very specialized in their regimens, as with the food pyramid, we may be better off getting a good mix of different types of exercise: aerobic (walking, running, bicycling, rowing, swimming), anaerobic (short bursts of exercise, such as sprints), flexibility (stretching, such as yoga), Pilates, strength training (weight lifting), and fun (tennis, bowling, golf, sex, snowshoeing, etc.). It is pretty well established that even modest levels of weight resistance training can help build bone density and help stave off osteoporosis (Layne and Nelson, 1999; Mayo Clinic, 2019).

Timing also matters. Exercising early in the day burns more calories, but comes with an increased risk of injury (Nazish, 2019; Robertson, 2019; Sato, et al., 2019). Exercising later in the day reduces the risk of injury, but burns slightly fewer calories. The most important thing is that you find the time to exercise and keep doing it.

Even with limited means, even if you can't afford to join a gym or play golf, you can start a really simple exercise program at home. All you'll need is an egg timer, exercise mat (a carpet remnant will do), music, and a pair of five-pound weights; if those are too heavy, then use three-pound weights, and if those are still too heavy, then start with a couple of soup cans. If even those are too much, then use no weight at all, and just go through the motions. Form is far more important than the amount of weight. Ideally, if possible, consult with a certified personal trainer to ensure you're using proper form. As always, consult your doctor before starting any new exercise program. If anything hurts, stop immediately, and rest, ice, and elevate.

Set up a simple circuit that you find challenging, but not so difficult that you won't want to do it again. The circuit will consist of a five minute warm-up (stretching), say ten minutes of exercises, and a five minute cool-down. After the warm-up, start with 30 seconds of exercise followed by 30 seconds of rest. Pick a mix of ten exercises; some examples are listed below.

Aerobic: Jog in place, jumping jacks, jump rope.
Core: Sit-ups, push-ups, squats, planks, Superman.
Strength: Overhead presses, curls, one-arm rows.

You can also mix in some balance exercises, such as standing on one leg at a time. Increase the number of minutes of exercise as your stamina increases. Take your time, no rush. Do as few of repetitions as possible per thirty second interval.

If this feels like too much, then start with just these three exercises: overhead press, squats (no weight), and curls. If you don't like these, then pick your three favorites. Do it not because you feel like it, but because you know you will feel better afterwards.

If you do only one exercise, then do this one: wall angels. I learned this one while doing physical therapy for my neck, but you can find plenty of guides online as well (Davis, 2019). These are much harder than they sound. Stop if you feel any discomfort or pain. Go slow. This is a great cure for poor posture and "tech neck." All you need is a wall and some non-slip shoes. With your back against the wall, put your feet about 6 inches away from the wall, and shoulder's width apart (6 to 12 inches), with knees slightly bent. Put your back and head flat against the wall, look straight ahead, and raise your arms straight out to your sides, also against the wall, palms facing out. Now bend your elbows to 90 degrees, so that your fingertips are pointing towards the ceiling. The backs of your arms and hands should still be flat against the wall. Now, just stand there, and breathe in and out nice and slowly, say ten times. Even though you're just standing there, your body is doing a lot of work. Breathing deeply to expand your upper chest and rib cage actually works the muscles in the back and neck. Don't be surprised if you can only do this for a few seconds at first.

If you can't do any of this, then maybe try doing what my dad does. In slow motion, walk through the motions, as if you're bowling, or fishing, or dancing, or mowing the lawn. Go nice and slow. At least you're moving, and it's a little bit fun.

Ideally, whatever you do, keep it fun. Not only does it make it more likely that you'll keep at it, there are also boatloads of studies on all the positive psychological and physiological benefits of play (Aucoin, 2006; Neyfakh, 2014; Seppälä, 2016). There is even a group devoted to skipping. I'm not making this up; check out their webpage: www.Iskip.com. It makes me miss my old pogo stick. Just because a body gets older doesn't mean we still can't have fun and play. Unless there is pain.

Pain. If anything hurts, then stop. Better yet, stop before it hurts. Whatever you're doing is not worth it; literally just skip it. In the first book, I probably said something like, "No pain, no gain," but I'm older now and have learned that some pain can lead to a very long recovery period, and possibly physical therapy. Avoid it if you can. Physical changes are best made gradually. It's better to start something slowly that is sustainable. The hardest part of all is starting.

While physical pain can limit one's ability to exercise, even more broadly speaking, pain – both physical and emotional – can negatively impact one's well-being. It's hard to be happy when you're hurting, and we are all hurting, one way or another.

Migraines, for example, can be debilitating and affect approximately 12 percent of the population. As a migraine sufferer myself, I've cut out a lot of the common food triggers, such as milk, chocolate, and alcohol, and I pay attention to the big three: stress, sleep, and hydration. There is new research by

Angela Stanton indicating that migraines might stem primarily from an imbalance in how electrolytes are distributed in the brain, leading to essentially the equivalent of an electrical outage in the brain, causing the classic pain symptoms (Stanton, 2017).

Migraine sufferers are characterized by heightened sensitivity to external stimuli, which puts a further energy demand on the brain. Furthermore, the migraine-brain is one that has not evolved to handle the carbohydrate-heavy modern diet, and glucose exacerbates the electrolyte imbalance.

Sugar is not our friend. Even for those who don't suffer migraines, it's wise to limit refined sugars. Fats have been maligned for decades, but sugar may be the greater culprit contributing to many health issues (Faruque, et al., 2020; Kearns, Schmidt, and Glantz, 2016). With its emphasis on healthy fats and protein, a ketogenic diet might help. It's worth checking out.

This is a gross oversimplification of very complicated things, but given the toll that migraines take on people, any research into understanding their root causes, and developing practical prevention, intervention, and treatment methods would be preferable to relying solely on pain medications. I consider myself fortunate, in that mine respond to over-the-counter medications, i.e., Excedrin Migraine.

The funny thing is that studies show that the more we think about our pain and dwell on it, even coming up with adjectives to describe it, the worse it feels (Hansen and Streltzer, 2005). Time slows down.

61

The best advice, believe it or not, is to acknowledge the pain, and then try not to think about it. Of course, the more you try not to think about something, the more you can't help but think about it (Lakoff, 2004, 2014). Let me re-phrase that: try thinking about absolutely anything else other than your pain. Re-direct yourself.

Note that this applies equally to both physical pain and emotional pain, as they are actually processed in the same part of the brain (Eisenberger, Lieberman, and Williams, 2003). Studies have also shown that physical pain can also make one more vulnerable to social pain (Chen, Poon, and DeWall, 2014; Lewis, 2014). Ironically, studies have also shown that over-the-counter pain relievers can relieve emotional hurts as well (DeWall, et al., 2010). Be careful, though, as these pain relievers have also been associated with decreased empathy levels, possibly because they act to deaden sensitivity to all kinds of pain in the brain, including our ability to feel other people's pain (Mischkowski, Crocker, and Way, 2016).

Want to be more empathetic? Read fiction. Numerous studies have shown that reading fiction builds empathy, improves social cognition, and makes people tend to be more helpful (Hammond, 2019; Johnson, 2012; Oatley, 2016; Tamir, et al., 2016). The theory behind it is that while reading fiction, the mind must imagine all the characters, and what they are going through, and to some degree, we enter their world. One of the best things we can do is read to our children. It not only builds vocabulary and literacy skills, it also builds empathy (Read to a Child, 2020; Snow, Burns, and Griffin, ed., 2013; The Annie E. Casey Foundation, 2010, 2013).

There is a free and natural pain reliever, and while mildly addictive, it's nowhere near as devastating as the opioid crisis. It's called swearing. Studies have shown that swearing actually provides some pain relief and improves pain tolerance, possibly by triggering fight-or-flee hormones that override the pain centers in the brain (Stephens, Atkins, and Kingston, 2009). The only down-side is that once you start, it's hard to put it back in its cage, and it's socially frowned-upon in polite company. Self-control takes work (Baumeister, 2012). Even though we sometimes encourage people to vent and blow off steam, we should be aware that we may be encouraging a habit that's hard to break. It helps to understand why it feels so good to swear, though. Use sparingly. Save for truly swear-worthy emergencies.

Breathing. When I took voice lessons, before I could learn how to sing, I had to re-learn how to breathe. In our stressful work-a-day world, we often fall into the trap of shallow, rapid breathing. We need to slow it all down. I took voice lessons once (not because I could sing, but because I wanted to get better) and the first thing the teacher taught me was how to breathe. It sounds like something we should all naturally know how to do, but here it is: breathe in deeply, smoothly, slowly, so that your ribcage and abdomen (diaphragm) expand, pause, and then exhale slowly.

Most of us use only a small portion of our lung capacity due to our shallow fight-or-flight stress-zone breathing habit. The best way to break this pattern is to take some slow, deliberate, deep breaths. Breathe in, count to three, pause, hold for three. Exhale, count to four. It's the fastest and easiest way to calm yourself in a stressful situation, and you can do it anywhere. Increase the count to four, or even five or six seconds, as you build lung capacity. Again, the power of deep breathing and meditation to induce the relaxation response is nothing new. Dr. Herbert Benson shared his findings in his book, *The Relaxation Response*, back in 1975. It has just taken a few decades to be accepted by mainstream medicine (Bender, 2012; Benson, 1975; Dusek, et al., 2008).

Weighted blankets. There is science behind the calming, swaddling effect of these blankets. They have been used for years now to help those with autism, and can also help ease everyday anxiety (Bestbier and Williams, 2017; Chen, et al., 2012; Grandin, 1995; Green and Rhodes, 2012). The deep touch pressure (DTP) works the same way as hugs do to calm the nervous system. I remember first hearing about this idea in the 1990's, when Temple Grandin, who has autism, developed her own "squeeze machine" to simulate hugging, and may have been the first to recommend weighted vests and swaddling for autistic children to calm their anxiety levels (Grandin, 1995). We now even have "Thunder Shirts" to calm our pets during thunderstorms. It works.

There are a thousand other little ways to comfort ourselves. Even just putting our hands together helps bring calm. I remember hearing once that when babies learn how to do this, they are organizing their world, discovering that their independent hands and arms are actually part of them, and all connected. Close your eyes, and do this now. Stretch your arms out wide, and then bring your hands together, palms facing each other, as if in prayer. You can feel both your breathing and heart rate slow a little bit. It almost feels like you're completing an electrical circuit. It feels good. It's grounding.

In some meditative practices, hands are extended, palms open up to the sky, which is a different feeling entirely, as though trying to connect with the wide openness of the universe. In body language, holding one's palms up always implies an openness and vulnerability.

When someone clasps their hands together, fingers interlaced, it's widely interpreted to mean that they're stressed, anxious, or frustrated, as this body language implies that they're trying to soothe or comfort themselves by bringing their hands together, much as we did when we were babies.

On the other hand, when people put their hands together in front of them, fingertips pointing up and touching each other, this is called "steepling," and sends a message of great confidence. Picture Montgomery Burns on *The Simpsons*, scheming to take over the town.

Singing. If you can breathe, you can sing. Studies have found that singing activates more and different parts of the brain all at once, and that memories associated with music get stored in an area of the brain that is spared by Alzheimer's due to its precise location within the brain (ventral pre-supplementary motor area and caudal anterior cingulate gyrus) (Jacobsen, et al., 2015).

I have borne witness to this first-hand, visiting my mom at the nursing home on concert nights. The band would invariably end the show with either the national anthem, "The Star-Spangled Banner," or "America the Beautiful," or both, and every time the entire room full of residents would join in. Some of them no longer recognized their own children or spouses, and were losing grasp even of who they themselves were, but they still knew every word of these songs. I am certain these familiar songs from deep within their memory brought them some comfort. I am pretty sure one of the best things we can do is ensure there is music and singing in nursing homes.

Singing can put us all into a happier mood. To quote Cervantes:

Quien canta, sus males espanta.

This translates roughly to:

He who sings, scares all his troubles away.

It is admittedly taken out of context, but it still rings true. The irony is that I am suggesting that we sing, to feel better, even if/when we don't feel like singing. The trick is that we might have to *act* happier before we actually *feel* happier. This is especially true of the next tip.

Smiling. The physical act of smiling, even if done intentionally, mechanically, even when you don't feel like smiling, still releases the same chemicals in your body that affect mood and make you feel happier (Riggio, 2012). Ditto for laughing. Usually we think of smiling and laughing as reactions, things we do in response to external stimuli that we find pleasant or amusing. The funny thing is that it works both ways, with or without it. External stimuli can create a chain reaction, resulting in the smile/laugh response, which in turn leads to the pleasurable feeling of happiness. It turns out that, even without the external stimuli, we can replace it with the deliberate conscious decision to smile or laugh, which automatically and naturally triggers the release of the good stuff – dopamine, endorphins, and serotonin – resulting in the same positive boost in mood. If we *act* happy, we might actually *feel* happier as a result.

It was in my early years as a supervisor that I read this article, and so I gave it a try. It actually took work! I had not realized how set my face had become, as my smile muscles had literally fallen out of shape. It made me remember the old saying from when we were kids: If you keep making that face, it's going to get stuck and freeze that way. Yipes, it was really happening. It felt like my face was going to crack and break. And so I decided I would remind myself to smile on my way into work each day. As I now always say:

The most important thing I put on every morning is the smile on my face!

Another crazy thing about smiling and laughing is that they're contagious. The mere act of seeing someone else smiling or laughing can prompt us to do the same, through some subconscious mirroring mechanism the brain uses to feel what others are feeling (Warren, et al, 2006; Wood, et al, 2016). Someone can literally have an infectious smile or laugh. The old sitcoms back in the 1960's and 1970's had this figured out, using laugh tracks to capitalize on this understanding of the human psyche.

There are many studies out there showing the health benefits of laughter, not only through the release of the feel-good brain chemicals, but also as a physical exercise. It turns out that a good belly laugh works a lot of muscles, and might even help with getting rid of some belly fat. Try to find something to laugh about every day.

Remember that both happiness and stress can be contagious. A conscious decision on your part – to smile or laugh – can not only make you feel better, but can also have a positive ripple effect on others. Once again, we are as impressionable as jellyfish, soaking up all the light, color, and flavors of the ocean in which we swim. Thus, it makes sense to pay attention to the company we keep, as the moods and perspectives of others can rub off on us and affect the emotional Feng Shui of the living rooms in our minds.

7. Mind Over Matter

Is happiness like the muse, something that comes to visit us, fleeting, comes and goes, without our control? Or can we somehow generate more happiness ourselves, through some sleight of hand, a thousand little conscious and deliberate acts to trick our brains to fall into happiness? Is happiness a choice? And if so, who wouldn't want to be a trifle bit happier? A lot happier? Our country was founded on the pursuit of it, after all.

If you think it's something you have some control over conjuring up, and it is not delivered by some mysterious magical gift fairy that visits and vanishes away, then you've already taken both a small step and a giant leap down the road to happiness. All of these efforts to change your environment to shift your mood reflect an attempt to exercise control, which is a central theme in the field of positive psychology. Here is the punch line: people who exert control in their lives, or even just *think* they are having some control over their destiny, are skewed to being more optimistic (Seligman, 1990). When good things happen to an optimist, they take all the credit. When bad things happen, it's just a fluke, just bad luck, and not their fault, and not a reflection of their inner self worth. Just by believing this, it becomes more likely that this becomes true, and they move on, past this rough patch.

It's fair to say that optimists are also a bit less grounded in reality, but reality is over-rated. The pessimist's better accuracy in comprehending reality comes at a hefty price. Optimists have more fun. If you want to become a little more optimistic, then I suggest you read Martin E. P. Seligman's book, *Learned Optimism*. It was a landmark work when it came out in 1990, and he is now widely regarded as the father of the positive psychology movement.

Similar to happiness, optimism can also be shifted a few ticks by consciously changing how you frame the world, and learning to shift your inner dialogue. It probably can't be changed one hundred percent, but can be by degree. In a similar way, while much of this book so far has focused on changing one's physical surroundings and actions to induce increased happiness, the remainder will look at how we can change our lens, i.e., the way we observe the world we live in and how we interpret all of our everyday life experiences.

It is not necessarily that easy or simple. If change is about exerting control and taking deliberate actions to become happier, then who wouldn't want to do that, if they could? The simple answer is that not everyone can. I would argue that the truly clinically depressed person has had the ability to make this choice stripped away, and stolen from them. The hole they are in is so deep that they can no longer see a way out. Once in, it's hard to get out, and professional help is needed. They need a boost, a helping hand to pull them out. There is no shame in this. The advice in this book is intended for the day-to-day garden-variety unhappiness ruts, but maybe it helps lift people enough that they avoid falling into the deep wells of depression. Just as with physical pain, it's important to act early, before the pain can set in and take hold.

Emotional ruts are easy enough to fall into, and equally difficult to pull out of, once entrenched. Even artificial intelligence has experienced this same phenomenon, getting stuck in a rut of negative thinking. A neuroscientist, Greg J. Siegle, accidentally left a program running overnight, and when he returned the next morning, he discovered that it had become stuck in a negative routine, and was classifying everything as "bad" (Petersen, 2013). The analogy especially struck home with him, as a researcher at the University of Pittsburgh, exploring alternate treatment methods for depression.

Likewise, people who are depressed are stuck. It takes the conscious, deliberate re-direction of thought patterns to get out of their mental/emotional rut, usually with the help of talking to a therapist, i.e., cognitive behavioral therapy. It helps to change one's perspective, if not by changing the scenery, then by at least changing the view of the scenery, forming new habits, and developing new internal thought patterns and an outward looking perspective (Bernstein, Heeren, and McNally, 2017).

If you listen to some of the music on the radio, and really listen to the words, there is a lot of depression, pain, anxiety, and loneliness in the world. Here are just a couple of examples: "In My Blood," by Shawn Mendes; and "I Wanna' Get Better," by Bleachers' Jack Antonoff. Shawn Mendes, with his big, gorgeous smile, is singing about lying on the bathroom floor on the verge of giving up. Jack Antonoff, who does acrobatics across the stage, has a line in his song about putting a bullet where a helmet should have been. Hey, are you guys okay?

Of course, as they say, "No one's always okay." Flora Cash actually uses this statement to introduce the YouTube video for their song, "You're Somebody Else," which has served as an anthem for those struggling with anxiety and depression (Flora Cash, 2018). This ache of loneliness is echoed in their song, "Missing Home," as well as "Hunger," by Florence + The Machine, and Ryan Adams's song, "When the Stars Go Blue," sung by Tim McGraw, and countless others. So many people can relate to this music. There is a world of hurt out there, crying out for help.

As our understanding of the brain evolves, as well as that of the underlying mechanisms of depression, promising new treatments, such as magnetic stimulation, offer hope on the horizon

(Nakazawa, 2020; Petersen, 2013; Rohan, et al., 2014; Salahi, 2014). Hyper-connectedness within the brain has been linked to both depression and ADD/ADHD (de Silva, 2018; Jacobs, et al., 2014; Salahi, 2014). There is tremendous connectivity within the infant brain, but synapses get pruned within the first several years to improve efficiency, leaving the most-used pathways that reflect one's "hard-wired" traits. In ADD/ADHD, the pruning process appears to be delayed, leaving many more pathways open, which may explain the increased susceptibility to sensory overload. Anti-anxiety medicines reduce rumination and repetitive thoughts, but have also been linked with Alzheimer's, perhaps reducing the connectivity in the brain too much (Tapiainen, et al., 2018).

Researchers have found that light and sound pulses might be able to treat the effects of Alzheimer's disease and possibly other conditions, by stimulating gamma waves in the brain, based on studies in mice (Iaccarino, et al., 2016; Jones, et al., 2019; Martorell, et al., 2019). Gamma waves are the fastest type of brain wave and are associated with our deepest levels of concentration, cognitive function, and ability to focus. Pronounced gamma wave activity reflects a highly aroused or stressed state; reduced activity may reflect depression or ADD. The gamma waves in turn stimulate microglia cells that attack and break down amyloid plaques and tau tangles.

Microglia cells within the brain might play a key role in both maintaining and eroding brain health.

While they typically serve in a healing mode, under stress they become inflammatory, damaging the very circuits they're supposed to protect (Nakazawa, 2020). The science is still evolving, and more research is needed in this area.

Maybe my dad is right: "Brains are like snowflakes, no two exactly alike." Truly, the universe within.

Otherwise, over the years, people have certainly tried a thousand different ways to self-medicate in their search for relief. While we've gone through a pretty lengthy list of physical and mental tricks to induce a little more happiness, there are certainly plenty of other traps that offer only false comfort or temporary pleasure, and often have long-term negative consequences when used in excess: alcohol, drugs, food, TV, sex, gambling, shopping, etc. These things feel good in the moment, but in excess and absent of any human connection, they offer only temporary and superficial pleasure, and do not contribute to long-term life satisfaction.

We've just covered some of the thousands of little things we can do to invite a little more happiness into our lives, much as an Olympic skier will seek the best equipment and aerodynamic gear to shave fractions of seconds off their times. These are minor adjustments, tweaks, enough to bring a B up to a B+ maybe. They're worth thinking about, but first you have to get to the mountain. All these little things only nibble around the edges.

Time out.

There is a cautionary tale in all of this, in that multiple studies show paradoxically, the more we think about happiness, and the harder we try to be happy, the unhappier we might be (Ford, et al., 2014; Heid, 2017; Mauss, et al., 2011). So, perhaps we should just forget about everything in the first half of this book. None of that really matters all that much. Throw it out the window.

No one can or should expect to be happy all of the time. Studies show that what's probably healthiest is to experience the full diverse array of emotions, in response to what's going on, and that certainly sounds more relatable, and do-able (Lewis, 2014; Quoidbach, et al., 2014; Tamir, et al., 2017). One of the benefits of "emodiversity" is that it avoids the negative rut, and shows that the experience of negative emotions is temporal, short-lived, and survivable, building emotional resilience.

Let's start over.

Maybe all that really matters is being a decent human, a contributing member of society and the planet, and being there for each other. That's all.

We don't live in a bubble, or on a desert island, and we spend our days bumping into and interacting constantly with other people. Other people are a tremendous, tricky, organic, convoluted, and vexing factor in the happiness equation, in that we all affect each others' happiness. This goes beyond the contagion factor, catching happiness from the smiles and laughter of others, to actual human relationships, the complicated, messy engagements and entanglements with others that happen because we come out of our shells and care, as we are inherently social creatures, and need and crave this interaction.

In the largest and longest-running study of its kind, Harvard's Grant and Gluek study has been following the same participants for over 75 years, since 1939, to see how health and happiness change over a lifetime, and whether outcomes could be predicted from their youth (Arnold, 2019; Waldinger, 2015). The Grant study has tracked 456 people from the poorest neighborhoods of Boston, while the Gluek study has followed 256 individuals from Harvard graduating classes, between 1939 and 1944. The study included regular interviews plus health scans. Dr. Robert Waldinger, the current director of this study, summarizes the findings in his TED talk this way:

The clearest message that we get from this 75-year study is this: Good relationships keep us happier and healthier. Period.

Studies show that we almost always feel happier after spending time with people – friends, family, neighbors, and even strangers and co-workers (Etcoff, 2015; Kahneman and Krueger, 2006; Krueger and

Schkade, 2008; Krueger, et al., 2009). I first heard about these studies at a talk by Nancy Etcoff, titled "Driving Ourselves Happy," which was part of the 2015 HUBWeek program in Boston. Researchers used an unpleasantness index (U-Index) to gauge the effect of different life activities on people's moods. Across the board, people's moods almost always improved after spending time with other people, with the one exception being their boss; more on that later (Krueger and Schkade, 2008; Krueger, et al., 2009). Also, not surprisingly, the daily commute made people the most miserable.

The big take-away from these studies is that it's important to enjoy people, delight in them, and pay attention to them. If we do nothing else, but we do this, then we have done well. Perhaps happiness really is as simple as developing an outward focus on other people, and it is in this web of connectedness that we can find emotional and even spiritual sustenance (Ladner, 2004).

This is nothing new. We've heard this message about the importance of friendships a thousand times before, from *Fried Green Tomatoes*, to *It's a Wonderful Life*. It's why loneliness exacts such an emotional toll on people, as well as bullying, being ostracized, and anything else that separates us from the pack. Isolation is one of the harshest forms of punishment, with examples ranging from solitary confinement in our prison systems to shunning in the Amish community.

Likewise, it's never good to laugh at someone. No good will come of it. We know this from our own experience, and we see this message repeated again and again in children's books. Go read *Captain Underpants and the Perilous Plot of Professor Poopypants*, and you'll see what I mean (Pilkey, 2000). No one likes to be left out, or made to feel less than. Getting laughed at is so damaging, because it threatens one's very dignity (Hicks, 2011).

Other people are probably the single greatest factor affecting one's happiness (Pinker, 2014, 2015). People have the potential to bring both the greatest happiness and unhappiness, the highest highs, and the lowest lows. Joy and sorrow, disappointment and delight. Everyone is a mixed bag, myself included. Ironically, those we're closest to can hurt us the most deeply, when they let us down, perhaps simply because we expect more from them. It's wise to look at relationships on balance, considering both the positives and the negatives, and recognize that everyone makes mistakes. It's part of being human. People can't help but be who they are.

When we're feeling down, we sometimes feel like isolating ourselves, at the precise moment we most need support. In rugby, a player might run sideways, toward the sideline, to avoid would-be tacklers, but in the process, would also be running away from their teammates. It's true in both rugby and life: Don't run away from your support.

The fields of sociology and psychology give us some really, wildly simple, practical tips on growing healthy and happy relationships. To summarize literally decades of research by the great marriage counselor and relationship expert, John Gottman, and his associates at the Gottman Institute, here are two key tips:

1. Respond to calls for attention. No one likes to be ignored. Their studies show that the couples that stay together have responsiveness rates of 86 percent or better (Gottman and Silver, 1999).

2. Make sure your positive interactions outnumber your negative ones by a ratio of at least 5 to 1 (Gottman, 1999). The negatives leave a deeper mark, and so it takes many more positives to offset them.

I'd first heard about the concept of an "emotional bank account," where we make deposits and withdrawals in the course of our daily interactions, from Covey training in the 1990's, but I hadn't heard about the 5 to 1 ratio until I saw the work by John Gottman (Covey, 1989).

Other researchers came up with a ratio of 3 to 1 (Fredrickson and Losada, 2005), but then their math was later questioned (Friedman and Brown, 2018) in an apparent disagreement between the fields of humanistic psychology and positive psychology. Either way, I would put money on John Gottman's findings, based on his decades of practical experience working with couples, and I'd argue that a lot of what he has learned can be translated to other relationships as well. It's just as important to be responsive in your work relationships, for example (Schmidt, 2018).

Relationships are the beating heart of a happy, healthy life. They protect us from loneliness. They help us re-frame the events in our lives and maintain perspective. They make us feel like there's someone in our corner. They make us laugh. They drive us nuts.

Studies even show that how we survive and recover from a natural disaster will be determined largely by our social connections, our 'social capital' (Aldrich, 2012, 2017; English, 2015), based on studies in the aftermath of Hurricane Katrina in 2005 and the Fukushima earthquake in Japan in 2011. Much energy goes into building physical infrastructure, but we'd be well-served to devote resources equally into building social infrastructure. Other people are literally and figuratively our lifesavers.

What do we live for, if it is not to make life less difficult to each other?

George Eliot
(aka Mary Ann Evans)

8. The Bird Outside The Window

I've probably learned the most from the lives of my sister, Angie, and my mom, about the complexities of being human, figuring out what people really want and need, and how we can best be there for each other along the way.

Of course, what happened is that I became busy with life, and then became a supervisor in 2005, and my life went into hyper drive, and my sister, Angie, passed away in 2008. So, the last three years of my sister's life coincided with my first three years as a newly minted, harried supervisor.

The expectations of a first-line supervisor are ridiculous: captain, chaplain, god, doctor, nurse, social worker, mediator, referee, disciplinarian, therapist, cheerleader, coach, confidante, buddy, event planner, clairvoyant, and fortuneteller; one who is able to read tea leaves, read people, and predict the future. It must be the origin of the word, super visor, meaning one who has superior visual abilities, to see inside people's hearts, to see through people, read between the lines, and see the future. Another seasoned supervisor warned me that the first three years were the hardest, getting systems in place, and getting accustomed to the rhythm of the year. The first couple of years, everything was a surprise. I had all the advance warning a bug has of a windshield. I worked many long hours those first few years, and finally reached a point where things were manageable and I could finally start coming up for air.

That's an unfair statement. I have always had enough air. I was able to breathe, no problem. Angie was the one who couldn't breathe, born with only one lung, a congenital heart defect that never allowed for fully oxygenated blood, and as a pair of final insults, a severe case of asthma and one leg. When she was born, the doctors said she wouldn't live to be one year old. When she was one, the doctors said she would never live to see her teens. But she did.

These are the stories I've heard my whole life, almost family legend, as best as I can recall them. Angie was older than me, by almost six years. When Angie was three years old, my parents heard that it might be good for her to live somewhere at a higher elevation, while her lung was developing, and so my family moved to Colorado for about five years. There they opened a pizza shop, but that's another story, and they had me, too.

As early as I can remember, I always knew that Angie's life was tenuous, and she could be taken from us at any time. Talk about survivor syndrome – I was born with it. I didn't really understand this phenomenon until I saw the movie, *Ordinary People*.

To many viewers, it was possibly confusing that the son who had survived the sailing accident was so unhappy. Shouldn't he just be glad he was alive?

I got it right away. Bingo. It could've just as easily been me, instead of Angie. Why couldn't it have been me? My God, thank God it's not me. I would never have been as strong as Angie. I felt so lucky, blessed, helpless, hopeless, and maybe even hapless too. I did nothing to deserve my good health. It was just luck.

So, that's my stuff, what I've carried with me, what is part of me, and has colored and informed my lens into the world, and why I can't not think about how it must be for other people, and why I hate leaving people out. There were a lot of things Angie wasn't able to do, and a lot that she missed out on. I thought about that a lot, and felt bad because I was able to do so much. This was my stuff. What I eventually learned was that my stuff was not her stuff.

I didn't start to understand this until her eulogy, when her good friend, Gary, talked about when he first met her, and wondering how she had lost her leg, imagining that it had happened during some adventure gone wrong, such as a skiing accident, he recalled asking her what had happened. She explained that she was essentially born that way, and that her leg hadn't formed properly and so the doctors recommended amputating it when she was a toddler, so she could learn to walk with a prosthetic leg. Angie's artificial leg was the most visible of her differences, but while it held her back from sports and playing with other kids, in a lot of ways, it was the least of her health concerns.

Then Gary had asked Angie, didn't she ever look at what the others could do and get upset, because she couldn't do what everyone else did? Angie replied with a question: "Do you look out the window at the birds and get upset because you can't fly?" Of course not. She viewed herself as simply living with the body she had been given, the hand she had been dealt. It could do what it could do, some things better than others. She didn't have a problem with it. The problem was all mine. I was the bird, you see. And I was constantly looking back through that window at the girl who couldn't breathe, and couldn't run. A fine time to learn this, at her funeral, graveside, on a frigid January afternoon, during her eulogy. A little late. All my life I had grappled with the fact that I couldn't fix things, I couldn't give her a new heart, lung, or leg.

Funerals are such strange affairs anyway. You're so wracked by sorrow, and yet you look to find the smallest of blessings, unexpected sources of comfort, and even humor, in even the tiniest of things.

For example, we were at the funeral home trying to make arrangements, and were having trouble finding a time and date when the priest was available. Mind you, Angie had left a letter laying out her final wishes ("When I have gone to the great beyond..."), specifically requesting this particular priest from her high school days, and he wasn't available either morning, though he might be available Friday afternoon, but generally it's not done, people don't hold funerals in the afternoon. Thank goodness Susan was there to ask the question, "Why?" It turns out that if you hold it in the afternoon, then you have to pay the cemetery workers overtime. "Well, how much is that?" I asked. It was $85 per hour. Now, realize, we had just picked out a casket, a reasonable one, not over the top by any means, which cost more than my first car. Paying the cemetery workers was a small price to pay, to be able to carry out her final wishes, and so that's what we did, we had an atypical Friday afternoon funeral, which in a way was fitting, as not much about Angie was typical at all.

Enough about her death, more about her life.

My sister packed a whole lot of living into her almost 51 years of life. Yes, she made it to 50, and this, after doctors gave her only 50/50 chances of surviving when she was young and pregnant. She survived. The baby survived. She was a mother, and a grandmother. My sister lived to see the births of her two grandchildren, who were the apples of her eye. She found love and had an array of wonderful friends. She went back to school and got a degree in substance abuse counseling. She volunteered and answered the phones at the local suicide prevention crisis line. She truly was a lifesaver.

She was wise in ways that most people wouldn't understand. Maybe it was from being so near the brink of death so many times herself, that she seemed to have a foot in both worlds, here and the afterlife. Just as they say that when one sense is diminished, the others become sharper, in Angie's case, if her physical abilities were diminished, her spiritual and emotional acuity was heightened. She seemed to communicate and commune on wavelengths beyond the sensory range of most mortals.

We were very different.

And I did what all birds do, I flew away, farther and farther each time, finally landing in Boston. I had my own reasons. Being gay and working in southern Illinois in the 1980's, I did what a lot of others did, and fled to a coast, a social refugee. But with that freedom, came the weight, the guilt of leaving my family.

Everything came at a price. Every action has impacts, ripple effects, and reverberations. There is nothing that we do that doesn't somehow also always affect other people. It's horrible. In my case, I know I hurt Angie and my mom a lot, in different ways, when I moved away. It was also what I chose to do, for my own survival, and to make my own way in the world. I was feeling abundantly hopeless and helpless already, unable to fix things, and since things seemed futile already, what did it matter? There's a certain fatalism that sets in, but it's wrong-minded, and I know that now.

The fact that you can't make things 100 percent better or whole, doesn't mean you shouldn't try to make things better, even just a little bit better. Other people aren't necessarily expecting or asking for a total life-changing experience. My sister didn't expect me to fix everything. I couldn't give her a new heart, but I could listen, be a friend, get Thai food together, and then hot Krispy Kreme afterwards. Hot Now! We could go to concerts together, see the Grateful Dead in Wisconsin, or Kathy Mattea in Joliet. That's what she wanted, all she wanted, to be treated as an equal. I could do that. I did do that, but I always felt like it could never be enough. That's on me, though.

I couldn't completely fix her, but I could make things a little better.

There's the old saying: "Always try to leave things a little nicer than how you found them." One time at work, all the regular conference rooms were booked, and so we asked for permission to use the executive conference room. When we came in, the room was a bit of a mess, with chairs strewn about. When we had finished, some of the people started to walk out, when I stopped them, and asked them to help tidy up the room before we left. They asked, "Why? We've picked up everything we brought in with us. The room was like this when we came in, why should we be the ones to tidy it up?" I responded, "Because we should always try to leave things a little nicer than how we found them." This is true whether it's a conference room or a planet.

A little nicer is do-able. Big change can feel too overwhelming, a bridge too far. This is one of the best lessons I learned from Angie. Through her work as a substance abuse counselor, she would say, "You have to meet people where they are." You have to enter the other person's world a bit to understand where they are and what is within reach for them. Being sober or clean even one day might be all that someone can handle, and even that might be hard enough. If it's hard to imagine one day sober, then talking about white picket fences and a completely clean and sober lifestyle is probably too much to aim for, and you risk losing them entirely. Thus, the "one day at a time" mantra. It's good to dream big, but be careful of overwhelming people in the process.

When I was in graduate school, I had completed all my coursework but still needed to submit a thesis to get my Master's degree. I had even run all the tests in the laboratory, but the problem was that I didn't know what to make of the data. I literally carried around this box of data with me for years, as I moved from apartment to apartment. (Not to be confused with a "Box of Rain," which I also listened to a lot in grad school, thanks to a Grateful Dead mix tape my sister made for me.) I had no idea if I was ever going to actually finish it. I remember this wall hanging I had (and still have) with the Chinese proverb on it:

The journey of a thousand miles begins with a single step.

It took seven years, but the hardest part was starting. I really didn't know where to begin, or what

I was going to say. The best advice I got was, instead of trying to write the whole thing, cover to cover, to start with writing about what I knew. I started with chapter two, describing my testing methods. That I knew. Explaining why the test results did what they did? That was beyond me, but I could at least start summarizing the data in chapter three, describing the series of experiments I ran and the parameters that were varied, which led to creating a variety of graphs and plots to compare the different test results. It was by playing around with different ways to plot and compare the data that I started gaining insights into what was happening over the course of the experiments, and could finally start to explain the results. But I never would have gotten to that point if I hadn't started somewhere, with what I knew, what was do-able. I had to meet myself where I was.

Meeting people where they are applies to problems both large and small, from the Master's thesis that loomed monumental to me personally, to all the world's greatest problems: hunger, poverty, disease, refugees. The challenge is, how do you get people impassioned enough to help, without overwhelming them? If you think about the number of people going to bed hungry tonight, or lying in pain and suffering (millions), you will just feel helpless. It's too much to wrap your head around. I can't help millions of people. The natural tendency is to just want to curl up in a ball, throw your hands up in the air, and say, "Why even try?" It feels too big, the challenges insurmountable, like spitting in the wind, or bailing the ocean.

Relief agencies and non-profits understand this, and so they try to put things at a human level, at a scale that people can relate to. Instead of talking about the countless, faceless, nameless people who are suffering, they show you one real person's face, with their name, and share their story, and tell you how your donation will help this person. They need to break it down to something that now seems fixable, do-able, and convince you that doing something will make things a little better in some measurable way for someone.

It simply helps to build a bridge, throw a line, to span the gap between the current state and the desired outcome. Show some connection. Give me something I can do today to move towards a goal. Put that first rung within reach, so I can take that first step.

The problem for me, with Angie, was that the distance seemed too great, the challenges too insurmountable. I couldn't fix her or make her heart whole again. I was the bird outside, and Angie was the girl on the other side of the window.

9. Focus On What You Can Do!

The second big lesson I learned from Angie came from how she always focused on what she *could* do, and not what she couldn't. She didn't compare herself to the bird outside her window that could fly. Again, with her physical disabilities, it always seemed as if she was more attuned to the emotional and spiritual spheres. She struck up relationships everywhere she went. At her wake, we were so touched when a woman we didn't recognize showed up out of the blue. When we talked to her, we learned that she was a taxi driver, and had often given my sister rides. When she saw the obituary, she recognized her, and was so moved, that she felt she just had to come to her wake. "We talked about everything," she said. It's what she did best, whether it was in a taxi, or volunteering on the crisis line, she connected with people.

This is good advice for everyone, in all aspects of life. When I became supervisor, responsible for managing and coaching staff on their careers, this advice again came to mind. The conventional wisdom was to try to fix people's weaknesses. If someone wasn't good at something, then that would be the thing the individual would get training in. In the back of my head, though, I recall questioning this approach. My sports experience would tell me to play to my strengths. You put players in positions where they can best apply their natural talents and succeed. In rugby, you wouldn't spend time trying to turn a natural-born prop into a winger or vice-versa. You wouldn't expend energy trying to develop a lousy kicker into a mediocre kicker. No, you would find an individual with an aptitude for kicking and coach that player into becoming a fantastic kicker.

In my first few years as a supervisor, then, the discussion of "what could/should be better" would form the basis for next year's training plan. I will grant that sometimes training is needed to fill a knowledge gap and ensure some fundamental competency in key areas, but it's still a question of prioritizing precious resources, and – to put it in business terms – ensuring a good return on investment. Address the need, but do not over-commit resources to improving someone from marginal to mediocre. Resources are better spent on developing people's strengths and focusing on what they can do well.

When I read the book *First Break All the Rules*, by Marcus Buckingham and Curt Coffman, I felt totally validated, and it really shifted my approach. This book explores through research and statistics, "what the world's greatest managers do differently"; what customers actually want and value; what drives employee satisfaction; and why employees stay or leave. I know of one small business that actually gives this book to every new manager. The biggest takeaway for me was that they agreed with my inclination to just figure out what staff do well and focus on developing that. Devote your time, energy, and resources to your strongest performers. More good will come of this than from spending all your time working with staff on what they don't do well. Far better to focus on what they *can* do. Plus, it feels good to focus on the positive.

This speaks to the whole concept of change. Can we change other people, or at least influence them? Can we even change ourselves? We have all heard the age-old advice not to go into a marriage planning to change the other person over time, and this applies equally to any and all human relationships. Think about how hard it can be for someone to make a change in one's own life, even when the person wants to change. The idea of trying to change another person is an uphill battle, fighting gravity and all the forces of nature.

Fundamentally, some things are more hard-wired than others. The malleability of our essential core psychology has been the subject of much study, and is explored in Martin E. P. Seligman's book, *What You Can Change…And What You Can't: Learning to Accept Who You Are.* If it's important for managers to accept people as they are and focus on their strengths, it's equally important for people to be comfortable in their own skins.

Knowing that you can't change people, managers are better off taking a line from the old Billy Joel song, and loving them "just the way they are." If you can do this, you can be a great manager.

It's not that people can't change. People *do* change. Change can happen, it does happen, it happens all the time. Life changes people, and shapes them, whether they want it to or not. Life can leave a pretty deep imprint. There are still probably some limits on how far change will go, however, given how deeply our hard-wired traits are programmed in our brains. It's hard to overcome our internal circuitry. The proverbial leopard doesn't change its spots.

Even if someone wants to change, it can still be very difficult. Just as we talked in the first few chapters about all the little changes we can make, in a similar way, even just believing that change is possible makes it easier and a trifle bit more likely for it to occur (Lewis, 2014; Yeager, et al., 2014). The desire for change can become a self-fulfilling prophecy.

So, there are all the things you can do to point yourself towards happiness, but can you *make* someone else happy, against their will? Probably not. Trying to change another person is misguided, very difficult at best, and futile at worst. It's not that we don't have an effect on other people; we do. It's possible to use one's influence very powerfully.

Expecting change, though, will most often result in disappointment. Encouraging people to "be all that they can be," and realize their full potential is a far better game plan.

There is some irony in that I started writing my first book when I realized that I could not change my supervisor or my organization. As a new employee, having worked five years previously at another company, I came in bursting with ideas about how things could be done so much better here. I started submitting suggestions, and earned an entire shelf full of little awards for them. The biggest issue I had noticed is that there was a lack of synergy or shared understanding of what work the group was doing. Staff had little awareness of what else was happening outside their individual lanes. Whatever sharing or cross-pollination that took place, happened purely by chance, through random conversations. It's as if we were all walking around with little bits of a puzzle, not knowing how our ideas might fit together. I wouldn't have been surprised if a couple of us drove up to the same site one day, pulled in and parked, surprised to see each other there, having no idea of anyone else's plans.

At my former company, we had weekly department meetings at the start of each week, to sort out project priorities, and sometimes re-direct resources to make sure everything got done. Department heads were responsible for ensuring the company met all its commitments to all its clients.

Some might be sitting there doing the math, and asking: With all those hours charged to overhead, weren't these meetings expensive? All I can say is that private sector companies are in business to make money, and they don't do anything that doesn't contribute to the bottom line. In other words, it would be more expensive in the long run if they didn't hold these meetings. The meetings must have been worth it, in terms of improving efficiency, identifying and addressing issues early, and maintaining client trust by delivering on their commitments.

Maybe it was just an added benefit that the meetings also afforded everyone in the department a window into what else the company was working on, and an idea of new customers, new capabilities, who was busy, who had bandwidth, where there might be conflicts, etc. For me, it made me feel good knowing about all the work the company was doing. Knowing how my little bit fit into the big picture helped make my work feel more meaningful to me.

So, this was obviously such a fantastic idea, to hold regular office meetings that I just had to share it, so I wrote it up and submitted it as a suggestion. A couple of weeks later, our office chief called a meeting. At last! Yes, he scheduled a meeting: to discuss why we did not need meetings! I was crushed, though slightly heartened when co-workers (unaware I had put in the suggestion) spoke up at the meeting in support of the idea. One by one they were summarily dismissed, and the final decision was announced: we don't need staff meetings. I was so dismayed. I had been such a diligent worker, bright-eyed and full of enthusiasm. I had put my whole self into the place, like it was the hokey-pokey, and this is what I got in return.

I walked away from that meeting, went home, and that night I started writing the first book, *Go Forward, Support! The Rugby of Life*. I decided that I could no longer put all of my energy and emotional eggs in that basket. I always refer to this as my own personal *Shawshank Redemption*, in that I was digging my way out, instead of one spoonful of dirt at a time, one page of pencil-scratched paper at a time. As my fortune cookie once said:

> *Discontent is the first step in the progress of a man or a nation.*
>
> Oscar Wilde

Don't get me wrong, I was still a good worker, a hard worker, a model employee, maybe even exemplary. But I had to change my expectations of my workplace. I realized that I could not change my organization or my management chain. I had to just let go of that, or it would eat me alive. The book was a necessary outlet for me, and then after the book came the blog, which was good, too, but that's a story for another day.

So, a few years go by, my immediate supervisor retires, and the next thing you know, I apply for his position and am selected to step into his role. Now that I am a supervisor, I start holding regular staff meetings. Now, here's the ironic part. After holding meetings for a while, I get feedback from my staff that everyone really hates these meetings and they get nothing out of them. Big fat waste of their time. In hindsight, I was probably holding them a little too often, and it was a mistake even suggesting that the meetings might be beneficial to them. I was the one who needed to get the updates. Not everyone had a need to know.

So, I stopped holding the meetings. Why meet face-to-face when an e-mail will do? I started sending e-mails instead. Then I got feedback that the regular e-mails were annoying, so I stopped sending those, too. After a while, I heard back from a few staff, sheepishly admitting that they did get something out of the meetings, and that they found it useful knowing about the other work going on in our group, but, "Please don't tell anyone I said this!" So, I started holding meetings again, albeit much, much less frequently, say maybe three or four times a year.

I was also flummoxed by Nancy Etcoff's talk, which suggested that people are less happy when spending time with their boss. This was horrible news! I didn't know I could be having this negative effect on people. At the end of her talk, someone from the audience (okay, it was me) asked her what a boss could do to make things better. She shared some quick advice, echoing the importance of maintaining the 5 to 1 ratio of positive to negative interactions; emphasizing what you like about their work; showing gratitude and appreciation for what they do; and giving them autonomy. I had heard this before.

There is a great little YouTube video, and an entire book by Daniel Pink, both called *Drive*, showing what breeds successful work environments. In short order, he lays out what does and does not drive employee motivation and engagement. Money does not. What does: autonomy, mastery, and purpose. The video is fun and well worth watching.

Since then, I've given more thought to why people might feel worse after spending time with their boss. First, supervisors are in the unenviable position of delivering negative feedback and constructive criticism. It can be hard to keep that 5 to 1 ratio. Negative feedback tends to threaten one's own self-image, and can make people feel vulnerable or exposed. Everybody makes mistakes. Not everybody knows about them, but usually your supervisor does. When people get negative feedback, there's a very natural human tendency to retreat and distance oneself from the source and seek out friends to validate their position. Ideally, I think it works best when it's possible to take a collaborative approach in shaping and developing their careers together, in partnership, and then such feedback can be put in context of helping them attain their full potential.

My dad has proved to be a surprising source of counsel on management. "Well, Rosie, any time you supervise people, someone's going to hate your guts." Thanks, Dad, that's the equivalent of saying, "You can't fall off the floor." You can only go up from here. Any bit of positivity as a manager is precious icing on the cake.

My dad continued: "It's all about feelings, and how you make people feel. Treat people the way you would want to be treated." Once again, stress permeates our lives, if we let it, and I have to confess, I have let it get the best of me sometimes. I can be an ogre. Recall the study that found that even Divinity students were less helpful when they thought they were late (Darley and Batson, 1973). Plus, if it's lonely at the top, it's just as lonely in the middle.

Maybe supervisors tend to be more stressed and lonely than their staff, and the supervisors' unhappiness is simply contagious, and that's part of why people are less happy after spending time with them. It's just a theory. Since Nancy Etcoff's talk, I have consciously looked for ways to reduce my stress, and my workload, so that I don't lose my humanity. Admittedly, it's a work in progress.

There is some yin-yang to all of this, as well as cultural factors to take into account. I have often referred back to a quote by the Dalai Lama, in which he observes that most problems stem from a lack of awareness of our interdependence. In our work setting, we are constantly managing the conflicts that arise due to multiple projects all having competing priorities and drawing from the same pool of technical resources. There is tremendous interdependency.

What's funny, and illuminating even, is that studies show that emphasizing interdependence and the reliance on others can have a de-motivating effect on white males raised in Western culture (Hamedani, Markus, and Fu, 2013; Lewis, 2014). Not so for Asian cultures, where this same message fosters positivity, team unity, and cooperation.

It's hypothesized that white men in Western culture are raised to believe in their own individual power to get things done, i.e., "rugged individualism."

I don't have a solution to this, except I now realize I have to be more careful about how I frame things. It also helps me understand why some staff might be less interested in what others are doing, and what else is going on in the office.

Ironically, studies show that the most attractive leadership quality a woman can display is self-reliance, thus being seen as neither too weak, i.e., collaborative or interdependent (kumbaya), nor too bossy (Lewis, 2016; Schaumberg and Flynn, 2016). Doubly ironic, men who displayed greater self-reliance were viewed more negatively, as they ran the risk of being perceived as arrogant.

From where I sit, I am always thinking of the interdependencies, the ripples, and waves, and ramifications of every move. Life is a giant flow chart, and I like to look three or four steps downstream. I believe we are all connected, and if we work together we have the opportunity to come up with better and more creative solutions.

Ironically, a study by MIT found that workers – both men and women – were happier working with members of the same gender, but offices with greater diversity had higher productivity (Johnston, 2014; Schmidt, 2015; Silverman, 2014). It's understandable that same-gender work groups would have more harmonious interpersonal dynamics, with birds of a feather flocking together. Increasing diversity likely introduces more divergent thought, and more conflict, as well as the potential for more creative solutions. It takes work to listen, resolve disagreements, and incorporate different perspectives, and while it may be less fun, it can offer big payoffs in terms of results.

There are some big take-aways from all of these studies. Diversity is hard, but worth it. People feel more comfortable working with people who are most like themselves. Making room at the table for differing perspectives can lead to more creative solutions. Not everyone wants to hear that it takes a village.

10. Do You Want To Change?

It was shortly after my sister, Angie, passed away, and I had been a supervisor for about three years, and in the midst of my grief, I would often go to bed thinking, how am I going to change my life, so I'm not working such long hours, and so that I have time with Susan, and time to exercise. How? I remember feeling so tired that I could have practically fallen asleep on my drive into work in the morning, or even in the dentist's chair while getting my teeth cleaned. It was that bad. I knew – in my mind – that I needed to change things, but I didn't know how. It was just another night, lying in bed, and running through the same soundtrack, how am I ever going to change things, when I swear I heard a voice ask, "Do you want to change?"

I sat straight up in bed. Susan was sound asleep. Had I been dreaming? I don't think so. I had been thinking, so I couldn't have been sleeping. Either way, the question hung there in the air. My first thought was, well, of course I want to change. That's obvious. But did I really? My actions certainly didn't reflect that desire.

If I really wanted these changes to take place, I would have made them by now. Maybe I wanted change, but I didn't actually want to make changes, because I was still doing what I was doing, working late, not exercising, etc., and so on some level it must have been what I wanted. I was making my choices through my actions.

I had to own it, own it all; both my actions and my inactions. This was a turning point. I thought about starting a second book then, but life again got busy, not just with work, but my mom's health also started to decline, and so that change didn't happen then. But at least I started taking some ownership of my choices, whether good or bad, that by virtue of doing whatever I was doing, I was on some level making conscious or subconscious choices and decisions.

As my mom's health continued to decline rapidly over the next several years, and we were faced with yet more impossible situations and decisions, the one thing that became very clear was that there was no other place I'd rather have been finally, than with my mom during her final days. This, despite our otherwise difficult relationship over the previous years of our lives.

Things can change, people can change.

11. A Cascading Disaster

Where do I begin? How do I describe it? The term 'cascading disaster' comes to mind. It's typically used to describe situations where one thing leads to another, such as an earthquake that also breaks gas lines, resulting in massive fires and explosions that can't be brought under control because the water lines have also been severed, and emergency responders can't get there because of debris and cracks in the roadways, and the injured also can't be transported to hospitals because roadways are impassable. Or a drought leads to famine and forest fires, outbreaks of disease due to a lack of clean water, and a refugee crisis. When things fall apart, they fall quickly. Everything, you come to realize, is a house of cards that can be blown apart by the first strong breeze. Any sense of normalcy or calm is but a façade, a pleasant artifice, a temporary state that can be broken by life's cruelties with the flick of a switch.

For my mom, that one thing was some surgery that knocked her out of her orbit, disrupting her delicate equilibrium, and sending her into a rapid, ragged descent into assisted living, memory care, and the ravages of dementia, an earthly version of Dante's tour through the levels of hell. It was like a ride through a fun house, minus the fun, without ever knowing what was coming around the next corner, made all the more horrible because it was real, and not a ride, and there was no way to hop off. Not only did we have no control over it, we had no idea what to do at each turn.

And they were mostly turns for the worst, though we did still find occasional moments of humor and small blessings. The descent, sometimes gradual, and other times in free fall, was broken up by intervening plateaus, the "new normal" to which we would have just started to get adjusted to, when the trap door would drop out again, sending us falling again, spiraling down the chute. There would be some recovery and some improvements after these drops, but she would never return to the level she had been at before the previous drop off. We quickly realized that we had to change our expectations, and that returning to the previous plateau was not going to happen, it just wasn't realistic. The best we could hope for was some time and stability, at each new plateau. This was a one-way ride, going down, with only a few intermediate stops along the way.

And so it began. The surgery triggered an acceleration of my mom's dementia, resulting in a move from her apartment in independent living to the strange new world of assisted living, then "memory care," and then a nursing home, hopping a ride on a medical transport RV, and then arriving at a nursing home in the Boston area, with a few hospital stays here and there mixed in.

I remember turning to one of the doctors when I was at my wit's end, beyond my breaking point, and asking, "Doesn't anyone just die in their sleep anymore?" The doctor was young, and he looked at me, perplexed, and replied, "I don't know. We don't get to see those patients."

These were dark and trying times, and I was brought to the edge of what I thought I could endure repeatedly. Even through this all, even in our darkest hours, there were moments of humor to be found, the smallest of blessings we felt, in the smallest of victories, and the many angels who entered our lives, walking the earth, disguised as humans, who helped us get through everything.

The very definition of charity might be doing something for someone that can never be repaid. After all, if there is the possibility of repayment, then maybe it's just a loan, a simple financial transaction. There is a final act of charity recognized in the Jewish graveside tradition of having mourners participate in filling the grave, throwing a single symbolic shovel or scoop of earth, tending to the deceased in a way that can never be returned.

We were just a small part of a mass of people, suffering similar challenges and fates, all stumbling along the shores of an unknown sea, into uncharted territory, sometimes finding comfort and solace in a friendly face. There were so many things that just figured – that the day we moved my mom from one building to another would coincide with the hottest day of the summer, as we rolled her furniture and possessions, precariously perched on a cart, across the parking lot in the sweltering heat. But then, at the same time, we were so grateful and blessed that Angie's friend, Nancy, and her daughter came with a cart and helped us with the move, stacking everything up on it, higher and higher, until it soon resembled the Grinch's sleigh, and also mildly reminiscent of college moving day at the dorms, minus the dorms and the beer. Thank goodness for Nancy and her cart! And for all my cousins who helped with her multiple moves, from the house to the apartment and later into assisted living.

My mom had accumulated a lot of stuff over the years, something very typical of those born and raised during the Great Depression, and so we had to figure out what was going with her to her new apartment, what should go into storage, what were precious family heirlooms, valuables, antiques, or collectibles, and what she had been saving for the Great Garage Sale. Some items evoked wonderful family stories and memories, and other items looked like precious family heirlooms but turned out to be things my mom had bought at somebody else's yard sale with the intention of re-selling someday, at a slight mark-up, at a garage sale of her own. So, it turned out to be true, that they were *some* family's cherished heirlooms, just not *our* family's. Into the garage sale stack they went.

Of course, even with our best efforts and intentions, mistakes were still made, and I learned the hard, inflexible code of the garage sale world, the rules of which are inviolable. A customer came across an old Louisa May Alcott book that somehow, despite our careful sorting, wound up in the box of books for sale at a price of something like 25 or 50 cents each. My mom was working as the cashier, and she immediately cried foul, and tried to put the kibosh on the sale. I pled with the lady, "It was a mistake, this book wasn't meant to be put out in the sale. I will pay you *not* to buy this book!" The lady was intractable, saying that this was *not done*, that once something is put out at a sale, it can't be taken back. Too late.

I don't think either my mom or I have ever forgiven me for that. One part of me says, it's just a book, how much could an old musty book be worth? I've peeked around a little bit on Google, and it turns out, quite a bit, substantially more than 50 cents. I try not to think about it, it's just too painful. As it would turn out, this was just one tiny cut along the path of thorns, hurts, regrets, and indignities that were to follow. We were just getting warmed up.

There were good things, too. There was the day my mom called after she had gone to see her new apartment for the first time (yes, we took it sight unseen, put down a deposit on it to reserve her unit, while the building was still under construction; it was the fastest check I've ever written in my life), and she said, "I just went over to see the apartment..." Long pause, holding my breath, fear building that the world was about to implode right inside my skull, time stood still. "...And it was *beautiful*." I exhaled, on the verge of tears. I had done something right. By pure chance and luck, and maybe the contractor's getting weary by the time they got to the third floor, they had left the space above the kitchen cabinets open (instead of closing it off with a soffit), allowing space for her to display her prized cookie jar collection. Further evidence there is a God, and angels that tinker with things when you need them most.

My mom enjoyed many good years there in that apartment, still enjoying her independence, and making friends with the other residents. There was a group that would gather in the lobby each evening, and they would share stories and order pizza. I called them the Ladies of the Lobby. They truly provided some wonderful camaraderie.

Little did we know when we made the first move to the apartment in 2001, and then to assisted living in 2009, that we would be repeating this process several more times, continuing the process of downsizing a little bit more each time. In addition to dealing with her stuff, her collections of cookie jars, cake plates, and Beanie Babies to name a few, there was also my mom's declining health, which required keeping track of all her doctors, appointments, prescriptions, insurance, rent, and finances, ultimately balancing and keeping her checkbook, paying bills and all of that. And yet, somehow, in the midst of all this, there was sometimes humor.

Take birthdays for example. We had a little party for my mom's 80th birthday, but had to keep reminding her that she needed to get ready for the party, because she kept forgetting it was her birthday. By my mom's 81st birthday, she was in Memory Care, and one of the nurses, who had become very good friends with my mom, and was another one of those angels, had baked a cake for her, angel food ironically enough, and brought it in to share with the other residents after dinner. She lit the candles and everyone started singing "Happy Birthday" to my mom, except that when it came to saying her name, "Happy birthday dear so-and-so," the singing just trailed off, because of course they could not remember her name. It's like the reverse of the show, *Cheers*. Memory Care is the place where everybody doesn't know anybody's name.

Shortly after this, after my Mom had moved into nursing home number one in Illinois, there was a birthday celebration going on for one of the residents who was turning 105. The staff had decorated the room and adorned her wheelchair with bright blue balloons, bobbing and floating overhead. There was a cake, and people from all over the building kept stopping by to congratulate her and wish her a happy birthday. My mom and I were sitting nearby, both of us probably thinking, how sweet! After yet another person came by to wish her a happy birthday, the woman turned to her friend sitting next to her, and said, "I hope I die tonight."

I couldn't believe my ears, but that's what she said. I don't know which is worse, forgetting your own birthday, or knowing full well it's your birthday and hoping to die. It's not as if we get much choice in the matter anyway.

As we all know, we don't always get what we want, sometimes we may not even get what we need, and most times we just get what we get. And we got a lot of that. No one could have prepared me for the constellation of maladies brought on by old age and dementia that permeated and permutated through every facet of daily life. The TV shows and commercials make it sound like it's just a problem of forgetting the names of things, and so it's just a matter of buying enough Post-its and plastering sticky notes onto everything – chair, table, refrigerator, daughter. It's just so much more complicated than that, ultimately affecting every major system. It went far beyond forgetting the names of things, places, or people. It was her entire sense of people, place, and time that took on a dream-like fun-house quality (again, minus the fun) where nothing as she saw it was as it actually was.

She had hallucinations. Not just seeing things, but participating in a full alternate reality. She thought there were children playing under her bed, and no matter how many times I checked, looked, and verified that there was nothing under the bed, they would come right back. Nothing could have prepared us for this.

What was also just as crazy (and aggravating) is that my mom remembered things I hoped she would forget, such as, "Where is my collection of Louis L'Amour books?" Yet she forgot, or more accurately, could no longer comprehend things like today's date, or the date of a future doctor's appointment. It could be so aggravating. Here is how a typical exchange would go:

"Hi Mom. So, today is March 17th."

"If you say so."

It took me a long time to appreciate another lesson Angie had shared from her substance abuse counseling days: you can't have a rational conversation with an irrational person. This applies equally well to someone with dementia. Alternately stated: don't argue with a drunk. Or, in this case, your mother who has dementia.

There was one social worker who also talked to us, to try to give us a better sense of what to expect. She interacted with the residents, playing a guitar, and when my Mom would talk about her, even though she couldn't remember her name, we knew exactly who she was talking about, as she'd say, "You know, the one with the bling-bling," making strumming motions on her air guitar.

This social worker was the one who finally explained to us that we needed to enter her world, and stop trying to correct her or bring her back to our world. She told us to remember the three R's: Re-assure, Re-direct, and for the life of me, I can't remember what the third R was for. Make of that what you will.

When my mom would tell us about the children playing under her bed, we would say, "That's okay, they're safe, just playing, and not hurting anything, and you're safe too." Re-assure. "Now, let's go look at the pond and see what the swans are doing." Re-direct. We learned to re-assure and re-direct a lot that year.

It was around this same time we also learned to lie, a lot, just when we had to, such as multiple times a day. Being a grown-up involves both truth-telling and lying sometimes. Maybe it's not so different from the lies our parents told us when we were kids, to protect us and keep us safe, except that the roles have now been reversed. Folks with kids might already have some practice at this.

Lying was not my idea, mind you. We started lying at the advice of trained medical professionals: social workers, therapists, and other healthcare providers. It was the loving thing to do. Strange, because I'm not used to lying, but it was kinder, and far better than getting into irrational debates with my mom.

This might be another permutation of the "meet people where they are" lesson, and for my mom, we had to meet her in her world, and stop trying to bring her back into ours. It was too hard to bring her back into our world. We never succeeded and the effort left us both tired and frustrated. It was all just a little bit tricky, though, because we couldn't necessarily tell exactly what her world looked like on any given day.

Her agitation reached its worst when Mom was straddling both worlds, going in and out, back and forth between her world and ours. One day, on the phone, she said very calmly that she had visited with her mother that morning, they had talked about this and that, but also that her mother had been dead since 1957, so she couldn't have been there to visit her. She was aware of the disconnect, which must have been alarming to the last rational corners of her mind. As we were losing her to the other world, as she slipped away, the struggle became increasingly difficult, because we never knew what topic might send her spiraling off. Joking was dangerous, because she took everything so very literally. Sadly, once she was all the way in the other world, she became calmer.

There are no instruction books for this, and each individual's experience is different. The only guarantee is that you'll need to laugh, lie, and cry, and re-assure and re-direct. It's like watching your adult parent literally regress, turning each day more child-like. It's like the process of teaching a child to ride a bike, but in reverse order, starting with a ten speed, then a two-wheeler, and then adding on training wheels, and finally moving back to a tricycle.

When teaching the child to ride, there is the moment that you let go and let the child pedal and balance on their own. In the reverse process, with aging parents, it's figuring out the right moment when you need to grab hold of the seat, to catch them before they tip.

It's a delicate balancing act, knowing when to intervene, step in and put in more of a safety net or controls, yet not robbing them of their independence prematurely. It's heart-breaking, gut-wrenching, and nerve-wracking. As another friend put it, when caring for her mom, "I feel like there is just not enough I could ever do." The depth of the need dwarfs our ability to fill it.

It was also becoming increasingly difficult to manage everything for Mom's care from 1,000 miles away. It was different when we were able to have normal, regular, semi-coherent conversations on the phone, but as my mom's health declined, even this became exceedingly difficult. More than once, I handed the phone off to Susan, when I had reached the limits of my exasperation, at a total loss as to how to talk to her. Susan was very good at re-directing her. I started calling her the Mom Whisperer.

It was eerie, but somehow my mom's anxiety level rose any time I was traveling for work. It was as if she somehow sensed that I was not where I normally should be. I started traveling back to Illinois to visit her much more often. I was also traveling a lot more for work, too, so it got pretty crazy. There was one time, I was in Baltimore all week for work, returned to Boston Friday night, then flew to Chicago on Saturday to see my mom, and then to Denver on Monday for work, and finally back to Boston Tuesday night. There were some mornings when it took me a minute to remember where I was.

There are moments that stick out in my memory. There was the day I was traveling with co-workers from Baltimore to Philadelphia, when my mom's doctor called (must take!) at the same time they were announcing that our train was approaching. So, I'm talking to the doctor, with my old flip-phone crunched between my ear and my shoulder (PT to fix that later), lugging my bags down the stairs to the platform (heaven forbid they have a working escalator at the train station), when I'm jostled in the crowd, and my phone drops, skittering across the platform, stopping just short of the gap between the train and the platform, narrowly avoiding a crash to the soot-stained gravel ballast below. The call got cut off, but I counted myself lucky in that my phone hadn't fallen into the abyss, and I was able to find a seat on the train, and it was in fact the right train.

By the end of 2010, we had to move my mom from Assisted Living to Memory Care Assisted Living. What's the difference, you might ask? Oh, about $2,000 a month. Even as we were moving my mom into her new room in the Memory Care building, I realized that even this might not be a very long stay, and that I had better start scouting out nursing homes.

I set out on a tour of all the nursing homes within about a 30-mile radius. Once again, it was a little bit like visiting colleges, sizing up the value and the fit, ultimately hoping that your parent can get accepted into a good one. Except that, when it comes to nursing homes, when one calls and says they have a bed available, you take it. You really can't turn it down, hoping to hear back from a "better" one, because when you absolutely really need one, you can't guarantee that one will be available at that time. Best not to think about how a bed becomes available. Generally, the nursing home is the last stop. You would hate to be in a position waiting for and wishing for a bed to "open up." Bad karma.

So, on Saint Patrick's Day, we moved my mom, Patricia, to nursing home number one in Illinois. This would turn out to be a short stay, too, though I didn't know it at the time. (Sensing a theme here?) I thought I had everything taken care of, as she was in good hands, family was visiting her regularly, and we were able to talk and visit on the phone. All true, but then she caught the flu and her health further declined, and she could no longer figure out how to use the phone, even though we had gotten one that was programmable, and all she had to do was hit the button with the person's name on it to call them. Things weren't good.

Timing was particularly poor, as I was about to go on a really long trip for work, when I got sick, and Mom's condition simultaneously declined even further. I knew I had to do something. I canceled my trip, and as soon as I felt better, I started my tour of Boston area nursing homes. Just one in the series of many miracles, I remember getting a voicemail on a Friday afternoon in May that a nursing home (my first choice) had an opening. (Don't think about it.) Now it was just a simple matter of getting my mom from there to here. The solution: my phone, of course, and Google. That's how I found the medical RV transport company.

This was it, we were going long.

This was the ultimate Hail Mary; we were going long, throwing deep into the end zone, all the way to Boston. Believe it or not, there are actually companies that exist out there with medically equipped Winnebagos stationed across the country with drivers and nurses who can mobilize quickly, with the skill and ease comparable to any Navy SEAL or SWAT team. And, best of all, they take credit cards.

"You what?!" was Susan's reaction when I told her I had just booked the medical RV. "You just better hope this company really exists and the RV actually shows up." She had a valid point, but I was so far out on the ledge at this point, what was one more risk?

What worried me more was figuring out how to tell my mom about the move. How would she react? Would she remember? I was going purely on my gut at this point. In my heart of hearts, I knew she would have liked me to be closer to her, and it is only because of what a coward I am, that we didn't move back to Illinois and try to re-start a life there closer to her.

I want to be clear; I'm no hero, no saint. The relationship with my mom was clouded with guilt and regrets most of my life, but I hope I was there for her in the end. I had always felt so selfish for having moved to Boston so many years ago to make my own way in the world.

But, if we could not go to her, we could bring her to us. After the call from the nursing home, less than a week later, we were on a flight headed to Chicago, to talk to Mom about the move, and then (hopefully) pack up her stuff.

"So, Mom, there's something important we want to talk to you about. How would you feel about moving to a place where you could be closer to me and Susan?"

"Well, we'll have to..." Once again, I'm hanging there, suspended in mid-air, waiting for her to finish the sentence.

"We'll have to... live in a big house, and go on lots of vacations, and..." Waiting, waiting, and waiting some more. "And have fun." Whew! Relief washed over me.

"Okay, well then, we will need to start packing up your stuff and get everything ready to go."

Susan and I raced down to the car to get some boxes, giddy with relief. Another small victory!

"That RV better show up Monday morning," said Susan.

"I'm absolutely sure it will." I was pretty sure. "This is only Saturday. Do you think she'll remember this conversation by Monday?"

We went back upstairs with the boxes, to start packing, and overheard her talking to one of the aides: "My daughters are packing up my stuff because I'm moving to Boston," she said in a very happy and proud voice. So, the good news was that she remembered. Now, the ruse about referring to me and Susan as both her daughters was just her way to avoid any awkward explanations of our actual relationship. It was just simpler; this was a Catholic nursing home after all. She had used this ruse before she had dementia, too, showing just how deeply the awareness of societal expectations resides in the brain.

So, Monday morning arrives, and miraculously, so does the Winnebago, two drivers and a nurse, an hour early even. Our next concern is that my mom will have either forgotten about the move, or will change her mind. Again, miraculously, when we ask if she's ready to move, she says, "Sure."

We wheel her downstairs in her wheelchair, and there's a giant, 40-foot long RV, the size of an 18-wheeler, waiting for her. When the driver is getting ready to bring her onboard, and lowering the lift for her, he asks my mom if she's ready, and she just smiles and opens her arms wide. I could've cried. I probably did cry. I wonder if I am even related to this brave, strange, crazy, demented, spirited adventurer. I, myself, growing more cautious and careful with every year... Could I ever be so carefree, so trusting, and willing to venture forth into the absolute unknown? As luck would have it, a dear friend of my mom's was available to make the trip with her, offering the comfort and familiarity of her company along the way.

Once the RV embarked, Susan and I went back to our rental car, to head to the airport to fly back to Boston. In another one of those freaky, chance things, the car parked next to us had as its license plate: ANGIE. My sister's name. What are the odds? We hoped it meant that Angie was looking down on us and giving us her approval.

It was strange looking out the plane window into the dark night sky, and knowing that somewhere down there was an RV rolling along, with my Mom safely on board. I was more thrilled and excited and scared than I thought I would be. Almost giddy. Maybe a little bit like what new parents must feel when bringing their newborn home from the hospital.

Yet what we didn't know is that we would face yet more impossible situations and decisions. Horrible as it all was, from it I learned not to judge others, and show some compassion for those who have struggled and failed.

This was – literally and figuratively – a really long chapter. We were eager to start a new chapter of my mom's life in Boston.

A thousand miles…

12. Boston

We woke to the sound of the phone ringing, the folks on the RV calling to let us know they were getting close to town. We dashed out the door to be there to greet her when she pulled in. It turns out she slept most of the way, despite thunderstorms in Ohio and New York (she always loved a good thunderstorm), but not before having dinner at a rest stop restaurant, and demanding they go back in to get her French fries to go with her hamburger.

The trip completely wore her out, and she slept like a baby those first couple of days. Finally, by Saturday, she was awake enough that we were able to visit a bit. At the end of our visit, I told her we were going home, but we would be back in the morning, to go to Sunday Mass with her, if she'd like to go. Giving us a curious, somewhat concerned look, she asked us, "Isn't that a long way?" Ack! I could see the wheels spinning in her head, wondering how we could go home to Boston and come back to see her the next morning – in Illinois - for church?

Prior to making the move, we had worried that she wouldn't remember our conversation about moving to Boston, but we hadn't thought about it once she got to Boston. My stomach sank, in sheer panic, realizing that she had forgotten the entire conversation and the trip already, and it was simply too big, too much to try to explain again. No good would come of it. Time to lie again.

"No, no, it's not too bad at all. We'll see you in the morning." She shrugged, re-assured, and went back to sleep. Crisis averted. It also didn't help when tornadoes cut through Springfield, Massachusetts that summer. It was all over the news. We get tornadoes all the time in Illinois, so it could have just as easily been Springfield, Illinois, in her mind. The external world was becoming less and less relevant.

These visits with her gave me a chance for closure on a few things. A while back, around Christmas, she had mentioned how badly she felt when Angie and I were little. She remembered one Christmas when we were so poor that she wrapped up coloring books for us. I realized she had been living with this regret for all these years, decades, and yet I had no recollection of it in my memory banks, and it had clearly made no discernible impression on me. I wanted – needed – to let her know, I had never felt poor. I carried no memory of hurt from it.

I took this chance to tell her all of this, that I just remembered having presents to open at Christmas, and all the great meals she would make for us, big ham dinners, garlic salad, pizza... Her gaze shifted, and then settled on me. Uh oh.

126

"Do you still have my meat grinder?"

This would be the grinder she used to make ham salad, and to make Thanksgiving turkey stuffing, jamming in all the gizzards and onions, dreadful to watch, but delicious to eat, it really is the only way to make a proper dressing.

Do we still have it? As I mentioned, we had down-sized repeatedly through the course of all her moves, and somehow a meat grinder did not seem like an essential item to have at the nursing home, so we had bestowed it on either a friend or family member, or possibly Goodwill. Does it still exist somewhere in the universe? Yes, if you could walk into the right house, or Goodwill store, you could find the shelf it's sitting on, and so, yes, we could still have the grinder. But I can't say this. Back to the R & R strategy.

Re-assure: "Yes, Jenny has the grinder, it's at her house, and she is saving it for you."

Re-direct: "Let's go over to the cafeteria, and maybe they'll have ham salad there."

Unlikely, highly unlikely. Ham salad is a Midwestern thing, *no one, absolutely no one* in New England eats ham salad. (Hmm, maybe they'd be happier if they did.) I was kicking myself, and just hoping she would forget about the promise of the possibility of ham salad by the time we got there.

But lo and behold, here was yet another one of those miracles: the café at the nursing home had ham salad sandwiches! Good ham salad at that. And Mom liked it. She ate her sandwich, and half of mine. I could have cried. I was beaming, I was so grateful. She could still chew and swallow then, but I didn't know enough then to realize that I should have been thankful even for this. I didn't know what was still to come. Probably just as well, as we got to enjoy this one moment.

In her short time here, she not only lived through the tornadoes that summer, but also a hurricane, the D.C. earthquake that shook things up the coast, even causing things to rattle a bit at my mom's place, and in baseball, the catastrophic collapse of the Red Sox. Neither my Mom nor the Red Sox would see October that year.

In just another one of those happy coincidences, strange chance, fate, or miracles, I heard this one song in particular on the radio only two times ever in my life, both the day she fell ill, as I was driving to the nursing home, and again the day she died, as I was heading home from the nursing home, a wasted shell of grief. The song was, "In The Sun," written by Joseph Arthur, but this was the Michael Stipe and Chris Martin version. I'd never heard it before, and I've never heard it played on the radio again since that day. It's the best song, never ever played on the radio. It just stuck with me, and I of course interpreted it as a divine message from beyond, and clung to it for comfort.

I mentioned this song to our local funeral director, the same one who had helped us with Angie in so many thoughtful and caring ways. She was truly another angel, helping us to get Angie's make-up done right (she would have wanted that). And she drives the hearse, too. An unusual everyday miracle worker, she downloaded the song so that we could play it at the funeral home. (Non-liturgical music is not allowed at the church.) She had helped us the same way before, helping us honor another of Angie's last requests, by playing "Let It Be." Returning to the funeral home just a little over three years after we had been there to make arrangements for Angie seemed surreal, yet comforting. Morbid humor, I know, but I thought maybe we had earned a place in the Frequent Diers' Club.

Funerals again are crazy. They involve all the complexity of a small wedding (songs, flowers, obituary, outfits, eulogy, luncheon), with only days to plan it. They're both a surprise party, and a come-as-you-are party for all involved.

When the priest asked us about which reading we wanted to use at the funeral Mass, I knew immediately just the one, the story of Lazarus. When Jesus arrived in Bethany, He discovered that He was too late, and His friend Lazarus had already died. "Jesus wept." He then raised him from the dead. Even Jesus wept.

What I remember saying at my Mom's funeral is that we'd miss her laughter and the love she showed the world, and that all love is God's love, and may

God's love be with all of us, alluding to the song that had book-ended her final days.

One of the ways my mom showed her love for us was by cooking. By sharing some of her recipes, and a few of my own, this is my way of showing and sharing my mom's love with the world.

13. The Cookbook Chapter

Brownies. I gave you a recipe for brownies in my last book. How impractical is that? You can't live on brownies alone. It figures, on many levels, that the first book, promoting an extended childhood, would have a recipe for brownies in it. Well, this book is about being a grown-up, which requires fending for oneself and even feeding others.

These first two recipes are the foods I grew up on, my mom's pièces de résistance. They were our comfort foods, made with simple ingredients. We had garlic salad almost every Sunday with dinner, and pizza almost every Saturday night, while watching sitcoms, like *Rhoda*, often capped off with a batch of my mom's fudge or Rice Krispies treats, and *Saturday Night Live*. Those are still some of my happiest childhood memories.

My Mom's Secret Pizza Recipe

My mom's pizza actually began as my dad's ma's pizza. There's a long story to this. One might ask what business a German-Romanian has in getting into the pizza business, but this is America after all, where anybody can do anything.

When my Dad got out of the service, he convinced a buddy of his, Phil Barcus, to open a bakery with him, which they did. Phil was a professional baker; my Dad was allergic to flour, but an eager entrepreneur. It was called the Bonnie Rose Bakery, in Plainfield, Illinois. Around this time, pizza was starting to become popular in the Chicago area. My dad's mom kept pestering him, telling him she wanted to try that new thing called *pizza*. My dad then pestered his buddy, Phil, about making pizza, and one morning my dad walked into the shop and Phil had baked about a dozen pizza pies, and basically said something like, "Here's your blankety-blank-blankin' pizzas!"

My dad took the pizzas to his mom, and they were a hit. Realize that these early pizzas were made with American cheese and Polish sausage. They started making them and selling them at the bakery, $1.69 for a 16-inch pizza. When they started selling better than their baked goods, my dad decided to open a pizza shop in Aurora, and called it Ma's Pizza. He met my mom, who worked across the street at her dad's corner grocery store.

My parents moved to Colorado because they heard that Angie might do better with her asthma and one lung, living at a higher altitude, and it was there that they opened yet another pizza shop. At least, that's the story as I have always heard it told, but I've often wondered if my dad's love for the Air Force Academy might have also been a factor. He loved the Blue Angels and the Thunderbirds, and a few of the pilots even came into his shop sometimes.

Dad named the shop there Pizza King. Sounds like Pete's a King, get it? Drove my mother nuts.

There was actually a lot more that drove my mom nuts about my dad, unfortunately. Things were hard there, money was tight, and we ultimately moved back to Illinois in 1965, driving through one of the worst snowstorms to hit the plains in decades. Back in Illinois, my dad had a pizza shop for a while, but then took a job that offered a more steady income, regular hours, and benefits. My mom took a job as a cashier at the local Thrif-T-Mart grocery store. Things were still hard. They weren't happy together, and my parents eventually divorced.

My mom, a struggling single parent, raising two headstrong (Angie) and precocious (me) daughters, still had the magic pizza recipe, and it served to feed us many a night, and made sure we never went hungry. We may not have had much money, but we never felt poor, thanks to this pizza.

Mom closely guarded this recipe all her life. Maybe there was some thought of either selling it, or opening another pizza shop one day. It was also viewed as our golden ticket, something to fall back on. But now I sit here with this recipe. Am I going to run off and open a pizza shop at this point in my life? Am I willing to put in the grueling 12-hour days to make a go of it? Am I willing to bet it all on this pizza recipe, when the world is already flooded with pizza?

And yet, if I hold onto something like this, that is so amazing, and could make so many people happy, shouldn't I do something with it and share it? I feel the weight of this responsibility. With great pizza comes great responsibility. There's no one left to ask permission from. My dad says he doesn't even remember the original dough recipe he used, proportioned to make it in bulk. All I have is the recipe in hand, written down while listening to my mom give instructions over the phone, corroborated with a single index card from her recipe box, with no title, and just the five magic ingredients for the dough.

It just seems wrong to have something this good, this wonderful, which could feed people and make people so happy, and *not* share it. So, here it goes.

The beauty of this recipe is that it enables anyone to make a delicious and inexpensive dinner, fast and simple, in their own home. But, there is some advance prep work to be done. I promise you, though, once you have some pizza dough made and everything else you need on hand, you can deliver this pizza to your own table in 30 minutes from start to finish.

The Pan. We always baked our pizzas on a blackened well-seasoned aluminum baking sheet pan. You need the right pan to get the crust to come out crispy. I've tried using pizza stones and non-stick Teflon sheets, but the crust always comes out soft and bready. I am lucky enough to still have one of these pans.

You will need to either season a pan of your own, or purchase a pre-seasoned pan (a few exist). There are various instructions for seasoning a pan; I've never done it. According to my dad, all you do is coat the pan with Crisco shortening (not oil) and put it in the oven for several hours at a high temperature (say 500° F) until it stops smoking. I can guarantee you it will set off your smoke detectors. It's probably best to do this on a day when you can open all the windows.

While our pans were all aluminum, there was some research in the 1960's and 1970's that linked aluminum with Alzheimer's. According to the Alzheimer's Association, researchers have not been able to reproduce the results, and the original studies may have been flawed (Howley, 2019). Recent research seems to indicate fluoride may play a role (Cao, et al., 2019; Russ, et al., 2020). This could potentially implicate the entire family of fluorinated compounds. If you want to play it on the safe side, then look for a cast-iron pan instead of aluminum.

The ideal size is 14 x 18 inches, yes, rectangular. The size matters because the recipe makes enough dough for two pizzas this size. If you go with a different size pan, you'll have to do some math and make some adjustments, to make sure the crust has the proper thickness. There are precious few pre-seasoned pans available on the market, and the most suitable one I've found so far, by Lodge, is round, and 14 inches in diameter.

Cake Boards. Before we start making pizza, we need to make sure we have something to serve it on, a landing place for it when it comes out of the oven. When I was a kid, my mom used brown paper bags, laid flat, and that worked fine. If this seems unpalatable by today's standards, then cake boards work well. They're basically clean, food-grade corrugated cardboard. The corrugations are key, as they allow the pizza to breathe, thereby keeping it crispy, by avoiding condensation, which would make it get soggy. These cake boards are sold at Walmart, with the other cake decorating supplies. They have some that are 13 x 19, which fit our pizzas perfectly.

Work Surface. The pizza shop had butcher block countertops, the perfect surface for rolling out pizza doughs, but my Mom did just fine rolling out her doughs on our old Formica countertops as well. If the dough sticks to your countertop, add more flour, or invest in a silicone mat.

Now we can begin!

Ingredients for Dough (makes two pies):
  2 cups hot water
  ½ cup Crisco shortening
  2 packages yeast
  dash salt
  4 to 5 cups flour

Measure out Crisco and place in a mixing bowl. Yes, Crisco. This dough is really almost a cross between a bread and a pie crust, and the Crisco is what makes for a crispy crust, and gives it its flakiness.

Add about ½ cup hot water. How hot? Hot enough to soften the Crisco, but not melt it. Use a fork to soften the Crisco in the water.

Add yeast, and stir with a fork to dissolve it. Let sit for 15 to 20 minutes. Add the rest of the hot water, a dash or two of salt, and start mixing in the flour with a fork, or a mixer with a dough hook if you have it. Add just enough flour to form a soft dough.

Turn out the dough onto a well-floured surface, and knead well. You might wind up working in another half cup of flour, but don't overdo it.

Put the dough ball back into the mixing bowl, cover with a towel, and place in a nice warm, dark, humid place to rise. Allow about half an hour to an hour for the dough to rise, roughly doubling in size.

Place dough back onto the floured surface, and punch it down. Divide into two dough balls, equally sized. Work each dough ball a little bit, folding it over into itself, until you've formed a nice, round, smooth dough ball. Each will be about the size of a grapefruit.

At this point, you could roll out the dough to make a pizza, or you could refrigerate or freeze the dough balls for future use. Wrap in parchment paper, and place in a plastic bag. Do not use wax paper, the dough will stick to it. Another option is to roll out the dough, transfer it to a pizza pan, and freeze the flattened dough to further expedite future pizza-making. I've sometimes layered several rolled-out doughs, using parchment paper between them, and then frozen them, to have several in stock.

Lightly dust the work surface and the rolling pin with flour, and roll out the dough until it is about the thickness of a nickel, maybe a little bit thicker. If you roll it out and it fits nicely within the 14 x 18 pan, then it should have the proper thickness. The dough should feel soft, smooth, slightly moist, and elastic.

To transfer it to the pan, fold it in quarters, dusting off any excess flour, and then unfold it on the pan. If it sticks, don't fret, it happens sometimes. Take it back to the work surface, add a little flour, and roll it out again. Pretend you're working in a pizza shop, and quickly, confidently rolling out doughs for your happy customers. It works.

Once the dough is on the pizza pan, it is ready to be dressed. This is a good time to start pre-heating the oven to 475° F.

Ingredients for Sauce:
   8-oz. can tomato sauce (1 can per pie)
   garlic salt
   oregano
   basil

Again, one could go wild cooking up special sauce, but this is all we ever used. It's meant to be fast and simple. Really, plain old tomato sauce. I even use just the store brand. No big deal. The spices are what make it work.

Spoon out the sauce and spread across the dough. If you're using the 14 x 18 inch pan, then one 8-oz. can of sauce will be just enough to cover one pie.

Want a white pizza? Replace the tomato sauce with olive oil. Equally delicious.

Next, sprinkle a little garlic salt across the sauce. Take some oregano in your hand and crumble and crush it between your fingers, to wake up the flavors, as you sprinkle it across the pizza. Ditto with the basil. Use a little less basil than oregano. Before adding cheese, there are some toppings that go best under the cheese, and others on top of the cheese.

Add these toppings (if desired) before putting on the cheese: sausage, onions, green pepper. My mom used to put the uncooked sausage directly on the pizza, but we usually cook the sausage ahead of time, and drain off excess grease. I prefer the onions and peppers finely diced.

Cheese: Now add the cheese, a good whole-milk mozzarella, grated. Use the skim-milk version if you want, but it tends to produce a dry, plastic-like consistency. Whole milk mozzarella will give it a creamier, melty texture. An 8-oz. bag (2 cups) should be enough per pie. My mom would grate the cheese right onto the pizza.

Add these toppings (if desired) on top of the cheese: pepperoni, mushrooms, olives, bacon.

Pop the pizza in the oven and you are 15 minutes from paradise. The bottom of the crust should be medium brown and crispy, and the cheese should be completely melted and browned when the pie is done.

Pull out of the oven, and slide onto your cake board, using the pizza cutter or spatula, and cut into squares. Makes about 4 servings.

Serve with crushed red peppers and Pepsi.

CAUTION: You will be tempted to pop a slice right into your mouth – but don't. It just came out of a 475° degree oven. Let it cool off a moment, otherwise you risk burning the roof of your mouth with molten mozzarella. This is the voice of experience talking.

Garlic Salad

I really have no idea where my mom got the idea to make this salad, what the inspiration was, whether she found a recipe for it, or if it was just something she thought would taste good together. This is just another one of those mysteries.

As a tossed salad, it's a communal experience, totally different from today's standoffish "dressing on the side" business. It's meant to be shared, enjoyed, and eaten together, all in one sitting. Both refreshing and filling, this can be a meal all unto itself.

Ingredients:
 2 cloves garlic
 garlic salt
 oil
 vinegar
 ½ head iceberg lettuce, cut or shredded
 ½ head cauliflower, sliced
 4 radishes, sliced
 2 stalks celery, sliced
 1 tomato, diced
 1 avocado, diced

To do this right, you will need a large wooden salad bowl. Crush the cloves of garlic into the bottom of the bowl. Add a splash of oil, and sprinkle with garlic salt. Mix and mash well together with a fork. Set bowl aside.

Wash the lettuce, cut or shred into salad-size pieces, spin it dry (if you have a lettuce spinner), and add to the salad bowl. Add cauliflower, radishes, celery, tomato, and avocado.

Make one pass, pouring oil around the top of the salad. Make a second pass with the vinegar. The amount of vinegar should be just a little less than the oil. Sprinkle liberally with garlic salt. Add a dash of black pepper. Toss well and serve. Makes 4 servings.

Serve with abandon. And breath mints.

Chicken Noodle Soup

This is a kitchen essential: Chicken Noodle Soup. I remember the very first time I made it myself. I was out of college and living on my own in an apartment in Springfield, Illinois, and I got sick with some sort of flu bug, and the only thing I wanted was my mom's chicken noodle soup, and so I called her for the recipe.

Ingredients:
    2 chicken breasts with bone and skin
    4 carrots, sliced
    4 celery stalks, sliced
    1 small onion, diced
    3 or 4 bay leaves (or not)

Ingredients for Drop Noodles:
    4 eggs
    flour (6+ heaping spoonfuls)
    dash salt

Put the chicken breasts in a medium to large sized soup pot. Add water to fully cover the chicken; the pot should be about half full, to allow room for other ingredients.

Add 3 or 4 bay leaves. Or not. This is a point of some controversy. I would swear that I remember pulling the bay leaves from the soup when I was a kid, plus you need the flavor to make the soup work.

But later, when this came up in conversation with my mom, she said no, she didn't put bay leaf in her soup. Angie was already gone, so I couldn't ask her. The question about the bay leaves is just another one of those life mysteries. I put in bay leaf; you can do what you want.

Boil to cook the chicken breasts, about 20 minutes. While the chicken is cooking, slice the carrots and celery, and dice the onion.

Remove the chicken, place on a plate to cool.

Add the carrots, celery, and onion to the pot.

Once the chicken is cool enough to handle, remove the meat from the bones, and dice up or shred for the soup.

While waiting for the chicken to cool, you can mix up the dough for the drop noodles. Break 4 eggs into a bowl. Add a dash of salt. Add and mix in flour a spoonful at a time, until it has the consistency of a thick batter or soft dough. The way my Mom described it: mix in flour until you can't anymore, and the dough starts to pull away from the side of the bowl. If you want softer, eggier dumplings, then add in less flour. If you add too much flour, the dumplings will be hard, dry, and stiff. That's okay, they still taste great. It just depends on how you like your noodles. There is no wrong answer or bad noodle. Don't worry, you can't break this recipe!

While the vegetables are still cooking, and the chicken still cooling, make your noodles. Take a teaspoon, and first dip it into the pot, to get a light coating of chicken fat on the spoon so the dough won't stick. This will help the noodles slide off into the soup. Now dip a little bit of batter onto the tip of your greased spoon, (mmm), covering say about the bottom third of the spoon, since they will poof up, and then dip the spoon back into the soup pot and shake it to get the noodle to drop off into the soup. The noodles float, and will double or even triple in size, like little clouds floating in the soup pot. Repeat about 30 times until all the dough is used up.

Throw the chicken back in, and put the lid on, and let the noodles cook, roughly 10 minutes.

Serve. Add salt and pepper to taste. Don't eat the bay leaf. Best with saltines and ginger ale. Makes about 6 servings.

If you are so inclined, you can skim off the fat, but why would you want to do that? As I have always said, the flavor is in the fat!

Chicken Noodle Clouds
(a poem)

Clouds
Like drop noodles
Or dumplings
Afloat
In a clear blue broth of sky

Spinach & Rice Casserole

I learned this recipe one summer while working in the kitchen at Children's Medical Center in Dayton, Ohio, except I had to scale it down to make 8 to 10 servings instead of 80 to 100. I was in need of a job, with only $20 in my pocket, and my roommate, who was actually a food science major, was already working there, and as they said, "Jane is just wonderful, so any friend of Jane's..." It's not the worst reason to hire someone, but I was pretty clueless.

I remember Jane's laughter at my stricken face the morning they told me to go ahead and whip up a batch of egg salad. When I asked for the recipe, they said, "Just make it like you make it at home." Jane was laughing because she knew that I never made it, ever, at home! Undaunted, I winged it, and actually got quite a few compliments on my version of it, as most (normal) people had never thought to put sweet pickle relish in it. Well, I knew it went in ham salad, why not in egg salad?

The ladies in the cafeteria were wonderful, and committed to making food that would be tasty enough to tempt children into eating, while still being nutritious.

Ingredients:

    3 cups cooked rice

    10-oz. package frozen chopped spinach

    2 cups cheddar cheese, grated

    ¼ cup onion, finely diced

    ¼ cup green pepper, finely diced

    ¼ teaspoon garlic powder (heaping)

    1 tsp salt (or less)

    1 tsp Seasoned Salt

    ¼ tsp black pepper (heaping)

    ¼ tsp Accent (optional; contains MSG)

    ½ Tbsp lemon juice (or more)

    2 eggs (beaten)

    ¼ cup vegetable oil

    12-oz. can evaporated milk

Cook the rice in advance. Thaw the spinach in the microwave. Dice up the onion and green pepper. You'll need roughly half a green pepper and half a small onion. When you are ready to make the casserole, preheat the oven to 350° F.

In a 2-qt casserole dish (oven proof) or your basic 13 x 9 x 2 brownie pan, mix together the following: rice, spinach, onion, green pepper, and ½ cup of the grated cheddar cheese; save the rest to go on top of the casserole.

Next add the garlic powder, salt, Seasoned Salt, black pepper, Accent (optional), lemon juice, eggs (beaten), vegetable oil, and evaporated milk. Mix well. Sprinkle the remaining cheese over the top.

Bake at 350° F for 45 minutes.
Makes 8 to 10 servings.

Options:
For low-salt diets, cut the salt in half.

Accent is optional. While it was used in the original recipe, it has fallen out of use now that many people try to avoid monosodium glutamate (MSG).

Add thinly sliced pepperoncini peppers on top, before sprinkling on the cheese, to add some zest.

The other thing I remember from working at the cafeteria was that in case of an emergency, whatever it was, whether tornado, flood, earthquake, you name it, we had one job: make coffee! The doctors would need it. We knew our purpose. I've probably never had a more clearly defined mission.

Chickpeas, Lemon Juice & Pepper Salad

The last of the kitchen essentials is a dish I created while living on my own for the first time and scraping to get by. I still enjoy this refreshing, filling, nutritious dish today, especially on a hot summer day.

Ingredients:
   1 can chickpeas (aka garbanzo beans)
   ½ lemon
   ¼ tsp black pepper

Open can and dump chickpeas into colander. Drain and rinse chickpeas. Pour rinsed chickpeas into bowl. Squeeze juice of half a lemon onto them. Sprinkle with pepper. Eat with a spoon and enjoy!

Chicken Pseudo-Cordon-Bleu
(Chicken Schmidt)

This is a recipe I actually got from my dad. He gave me the instructions over the phone, and I gave it a try, and it's really quite tasty. It's perfect for that first dinner-at-my-house date, gentle on the stomach, and makes for a great presentation.

There is a bit of prep work involved, but then it goes very quickly, and finishes in the oven, giving you a little bit of time to tidy up the kitchen, light candles, and enjoy a glass of wine with your dinner partner.

You will need: toothpicks, wax paper, and a meat tenderizing mallet. A hammer will do, just be careful not to damage the counter.

Ingredients:
   4 chicken breasts, de-boned and de-skinned
   flour
   spices: oregano, basil, garlic salt
   4 thin slices mozzarella cheese
   4 thin slices ham (optional)
   vegetable oil
   1 small package mushrooms, thick sliced
   1 onion, coarsely chopped
   1 tomato, coarsely chopped
   2 peppers, red/green, coarsely chopped
   rice (optional)

Chop onion, tomato, and red/green peppers, and set aside. Slice mushrooms.

Start rice (if desired).

Put some flour on a plate, and mix in a little garlic salt, oregano, and basil. Dredge the chicken in the flour. Take one breast at a time, and place it between two sheets of wax paper, with a cutting board beneath it. Hammer until it is flattened. Try not to get flour all over everything. Place tenderized chicken on a clean plate.

Sprinkle oregano, basil, and a little garlic salt over the chicken. Crush the oregano and basil up in your hands, between your fingers, to release the flavor as you sprinkle it on. Use a bit more oregano than basil. Everyone thinks it's all about the basil, but it's the oregano that makes the difference.

Lay a slice of cheese on each breast, followed by a slice of ham if desired.

Roll each one up, like a Hostess Ho-Ho, and then use three or four toothpicks to hold it together.

Pre-heat oven to 350° F.

Heat up some vegetable oil in a large frying pan. Add the rolled and toothpick-ed chicken to the frying pan. Turn until browned on all sides.

Place the chicken roll-ups in a 2-qt casserole dish (oven-proof), or your basic 13 x 9 x 2 brownie pan. Surround chicken with mushrooms, onions, tomato, and peppers.

Bake in 350° F oven for about 45 minutes, until the vegetables are cooked and sizzling.

Serve with rice, chardonnay, and romantic music. Remember to remove the toothpicks! Makes 4 servings, enough for dinner – and lunch the next day (wink, wink).

The next two recipes are perfect for feeding the crowd when they come over to watch football: chili and jambalaya. I made both of these, and had two Crock-Pots going, in 2002 when the New England Patriots won their first Super Bowl.

Vegetarian Chili
(3 Qt Crock-Pot)

Ingredients:
- 4 cloves garlic, crushed
- 1 onion, diced
- 2 jalapeños, cut in half
- 2 peppers (red/orange/yellow), diced
- 1 zucchini, sliced
- 1 yellow squash, sliced
- 6 tomatillos, peeled, cleaned and quartered
- 3 Tbsp olive oil
- 2 to 3 tsp cumin
- 2 to 3 tsp red chili pepper
- ¼ tsp cayenne pepper
- pinch of basil and oregano
- 1 30-oz. can whole tomatoes
- 1 6-oz. can tomato paste
- 1 5.5-oz. can Spicy Hot V8 Juice
- 1 15-oz. can dark red kidney beans
- 1 15-oz. can black beans
- 1 15-oz. can great northern beans (white)
- ½ cup corn (frozen)

Dice onion, slice jalapeños, and chop up peppers, zucchini, squash, and tomatillos.

In frying pan, start sautéing the following in oil: crushed garlic, onion, jalapeño. Add cumin, red chili powder, and cayenne pepper.

Add to pan peppers, zucchini, squash, and tomatillos, just enough to warm and coat them with the spiced oil.

Put all the vegetables into the Crock-Pot. Add the canned whole tomatoes, and slice them up. Add tomato paste, Spicy Hot V8 Juice, and frozen corn to the Crock-Pot and stir.

Last, drain and rinse the beans, and add them to the crock. Stir them in gently.

Cover and cook on low for 8 to 10 hours, or on high for 4 to 6 hours. Cook rice separately (if desired). Makes 6 to 8 servings.

Serve with good friends, tortilla chips, by itself, or over rice. We usually set up a bar of toppings for the chili: cheese (grated cheddar, or even better, the fresh, white cheese, queso fresco), cilantro, salsa, sliced scallions, black olives, sour cream, avocado slices, tortilla chips, and rice.

Note that I use only red, orange, or yellow peppers in these two recipes because it helps people recognize the jalapeño, as it's the only green pepper in the pot. Avoids any surprises!

Speaking of surprises, be sure to wear gloves and/or wash your hands very thoroughly after cutting the jalapeños, and avoid rubbing your eyes. If you should happen to get pepper in your eye, I hear that milk makes a good eyewash. Good to know!

This next recipe probably bears little resemblance to an authentic Creole dish, but it sure is tasty. It started as a jambalaya casserole recipe that I got from a friend, but I've adapted it for the Crock-Pot, and since it's a bit more soup-like, I call it Gumbolaya.

Gumbolaya
(3 Qt Crock-Pot)

Ingredients:
- 4 links hot sausage, sliced
- 1 chicken breast, deboned, chopped
- 1 small ham steak slice, diced
- ½ lb shrimp, deveined and shelled
- 2 tbsp canola oil
- 4 cloves garlic, crushed
- 2 jalapeños, cut in half
- 1 onion, diced
- 4 scallions, sliced
- 3 celery stalks, sliced, including greens
- 2 red/orange/yellow peppers, diced
- 6 okra, sliced, or ½ bag frozen cut okra
- 1 cup uncooked rice

- 1 can consommé or beef stock
- 30-oz. can whole tomatoes
- 6-oz. can tomato paste
- 5.5 oz. can Spicy Hot V8 Juice
- 1 Tbsp molasses

Spices:
  2 to 3 bay leaves
  ¼ tsp black pepper
  ¼ tsp white pepper
  ¼ tsp cayenne pepper
  ¼ tsp celery salt
  ¼ tsp paprika
  dash basil
  dash oregano

First cook up the sliced sausage in a large frying pan. I like to use a good Italian hot sausage, such as from Prisco's in Aurora, or DePasquales in Newton, but if you can find a good Andouille sausage, that's fine too.

Add the crushed garlic, jalapeño, diced onion, celery, and all the spices except for the bay leaves. If there is too much grease, drain it off. If there is not enough fat, add a little canola oil. Once lightly sautéed, move to the Crock-Pot.

Now add the cut up ham and chicken to the pan. The chicken need not be fully cooked, as it will be in the Crock-Pot for hours. We're just infusing it with the spicy oil. Add to the Crock-Pot.

Next, sauté the chopped red/orange/yellow peppers, just enough to warm and lightly coat them with oil, and add to Crock-Pot.

Add directly to Crock-Pot: okra, rice, molasses, tomato paste, Spicy Hot V8 Juice, and bay leaves. Add the canned whole tomatoes, and slice them up. Mix.

Add and adjust the amount of beef stock (or consommé) so that the liquid level is about an inch below the rim to allow room for the rice to expand. The rice will absorb a lot of the liquid, so do not worry if it looks soupy.

Cook on low for 7 to 9 hours, or on high for 4 to 6 hours. Add the shrimp the last hour. Makes 6 to 8 servings.

Best enjoyed with friends, football, and Bloody Marys.

When the student is ready, the teacher appears.
Theosophical saying (1800's)

If today you hear His voice, harden not your heart.
Psalm 95

14. Love Is God

Through these recipes, my mom showed her love for us. People spend a lot of time trying to fill in the blank, "God is_____," but what if we flipped it around? What if we just said, "Love is God"? What if we just let love be our God, and our guide?

What if we could live our lives, simply radiating love, and not caring what others think of us, not reacting to what others say, or how others treat us? What if we could be more like the sure ship, sailing, cutting through the seas, set on its bearing, and not getting swayed off course, even while getting buffeted about by wind and waves?

What if we could be more like Henrietta Stackpole, the larger-than-life character, the loud American, in Henry James's *Portrait of a Lady*? Ironically, both James brothers studied happiness, each in their own way, through different media.

The world would be so much a happier place, if we could all be less concerned about what others think of us. That's not to say we wouldn't think of others. In fact, thinking of other people would be the cornerstone to this happier world.

It's what we're taught to do as children, and then we forget along the way. Regardless of the specific religions or denominations in which they are raised, children are often taught to say their bedtime prayers, and ask God to bless the people in their lives. "God bless Mommy, God bless Daddy, God Bless my pet turtle, God bless my little sister..."

Sometimes when I go to bed, I still do this. I try to think of everyone, especially those who might need it most, and run through my list, sending out love and positive energy to each person: family, friends, strangers, and even – especially – those with whom I might be at odds. Even if you don't believe in a god, you can replace it with "higher power" or "the universe," whatever works for you. At its simplest, it's about wishing goodness and happiness for them, and not any specific outcome, given that we are such poor predictors of what will bring happiness.

And maybe that energy travels through the atmosphere. There is actually a neuroscientist, Eric Leskowitz, who has studied and measured the increased energy at Fenway Park when it is filled with cheering fans (Steinberg, 2012). What's most astounding is that it's measurable. If putting our hands together in prayer makes us feel like we're completing a circuit, much like babies self-soothing and organizing their world, then imagine the energy field created by clapping those hands. It must be as if sparks are flying.

So, maybe the positive energy of a prayer really can travel and land somewhere. Maybe it reaches some deity's ear. Maybe it lands nowhere, and just drifts out into the cold infinite solitude of space as pure energy.

If it does nothing else, it redirects your spyglass so it's looking outwards. By thinking of others, you have primed yourself for actually doing something thoughtful for someone. Thoughtfulness begins with thinking of people, their conditions, problems, needs, and dreams.

I would argue that defending oneself against thoughtlessness, and avoiding hurting others, even unintentionally, is the single hardest thing to do. It's the forgotten birthday, the person you neglected to invite to the party, the neighbor you meant to check on during the storm, the child you were supposed to pick up from school, or the friend you were supposed to meet for dinner. It's the call you forgot to make to let your spouse know you were working late and wouldn't be home in time for dinner. It's all the calls not made, the cards not sent, all the places we failed to show up.

The problem of thoughtlessness goes beyond someone being left out, and the accompanying hurt feelings; it also shows a lack of appreciation for our interdependencies. No man – or woman – is an island in this hyper-connected world of ours. The irony, of course, is that despite all the technology and various ways available for connecting, we may be less connected socially than ever before.

Recall however that interdependence is viewed differently depending on one's cultural lens. While Western cultures prize rugged individualism (it's literally how the West was won), Eastern cultures put greater value on cooperative efforts, where every individual contributes to the greater good (Hamedani, Markus, and Fu, 2013; Lewis, 2014). Those who are raised in more individualistic societies don't necessarily want to hear that it takes a village.

How does one become more thoughtful of others? In that question lies the very problem inherent in it. How do you think of someone you're not thinking of? While not actively, intentionally directing harm at someone, the failure to think of someone, even if not done maliciously or on purpose, can be equally hurtful, possibly more so. To think of others, and give of our energy to them, takes conscious and deliberate effort. To quote the philosopher Jiddu Krishnamurti:

To pay attention means we care, which means we really love.

The kindest thing we can do is show that we are thinking of each other. Hallmark has it right. Ingenious of them, basing their entire business model on this precept. People like to know that others are thinking of them. There are other ways, though, to breed and demonstrate thoughtfulness and compassion.

In some ways, the process of becoming more thoughtful is analogous to the tips and techniques shared in the first half of the book, all the ways to modify your physical environment and take action to promote, induce, entice, and encourage greater happiness and positivity into one's life, the equivalent of building bird houses for the bluebirds of happiness to move into.

In this case, it's about re-shaping one's internal mental landscape to create an environment that is primed, ripe and ready to be more outward looking. To act more thoughtfully, one needs to begin with a conscious, deliberate decision to re-set one's bearings and turn the ship, and think more about other people.

I remember thinking as I was reading the book, *Eat Pray Love*, when the author was in India meditating for hours each day, and wondering to myself, "What's the point of that? What good is that? How are you helping anyone, or helping to make the world a better place by meditating all day?" The Buddhist emphasis on meditation and the practice of compassion seemed disconnected from the real world. You can't eat thoughts and prayers; thoughts and prayers won't pay the rent, fix the car, or heal the sick. Thoughts and prayers don't fix things.

I have come around on this a bit. Such practices – meditation, mindfulness, compassion – put one in the proper frame of mind to go out and do good works.

The internal environment is like a field where the soil has been worked and tilled, and is now fertile and ready for the seeds of thought to spring into action and bear palpable fruit. It's the blueprint framing our actions. What's going on in the inside matters.

This conscious, deliberate re-directing of thought echoes the previous discussions of seeking out a happier state of mind, as well as re-directing an Alzheimer's patient to change their focus. We can change our outlook if we change our mind's eye, re-direct our focus, adjust our compass heading, and switch the channel on the soundtrack in our heads.

Just because it is possible does not mean it is easy. If it were easy, we would all be doing it by now, and we could all get along, and there would be peace in the world. There are studies going on all over the world that are trying to figure out how to use empathy, compassion, and forgiveness to reconcile world conflicts. One researcher, Emile Bruneau, conducted such studies using brain imaging scans, and found, as expected, most people in opposing groups had lower levels of empathy for each other (Interlandi, 2015).

There seems to be something about identifying with a group that clamps down on a person's innate natural empathetic tendencies. Laboratory studies have found that the more strongly one identifies with their group, the larger the empathy gap, probably due to the "us-versus-them" mentality, and thus the reinforcing effect of polarization within a culture.

Equally curious, when reading about a third group that was not relevant to them, study participants showed ambivalence, as the regions of the brain that process empathy (theory-of-mind) went quiet. They didn't care about this third party, and it was reflected by the lack of brain activity. Love is rooted in caring, and the more we care, the more attention we give a person. Thinking maliciously about someone, and not thinking of someone at all are probably both damaging, just in different ways.

The tough nut to be cracked is how to translate all of this research into social change, to bring down walls, build bridges between groups, and create awareness – and caring – for the plight of those outside our circle.

Donna Hicks is a pioneer in conflict resolution, whose ideas are encapsulated in her book, *Dignity: Its Essential Role in Resolving Conflict* (Hicks, 2011). Her thesis is that all human interaction revolves around dignity, the principle that every life matters and has innate worth. Just as we need food for our physical bodies, we require social validation to feed our dignity needs, to know that our lives have value and worth; that we matter. Just as everyone needs food to eat, one's very existence cries out for and demands dignity. Donna Hicks calls dignity a birthright.

Most conflicts of course arise when people feel their innate dignity has been violated. Anger after all is another manifestation of pain. Donna Hicks has been involved in conflict resolution in as far-flung places as South America, Northern Ireland, and corporate America. The trick it seems is for each side to open up and share how they've been hurt, how their dignity has been violated, and why they did the things they did. The goal is to get people to see the common humanity in each other, as individuals, and not part of some large faceless group.

Group identity is what triggers the empathy gap. People relating to each other as individuals is what closes it.

Problems have to be made relatable, bite-sized. If you want people to engage, then you have to tell individual stories that people can relate to. People have to see past the barriers of group identity, to be able to truly see others as individuals, who are not so unlike themselves.

In journalism, it is common knowledge that readers will get overwhelmed reading a story about something that happened to vast, faceless masses of other people (Allis, 2010). It's too much; readers can't take it in. They lose the ability to empathize. They shut down and feel powerless. Daunted by the magnitude of the world's problems, people can become numb, paralyzed against taking action. And so journalists make the story relatable, by narrowing the focus of the lens to a single individual.

Who can forget the image of the Turkish police officer, holding the lifeless body of a child that had washed up on shore? This photograph of a single child spoke volumes for the depth of suffering of millions of Syrian refugees, and sparked a global outcry. Isn't the suffering and loss of even one child, one child too many?

Granted, some days it may feel like we are bailing the ocean, but it doesn't mean we should stop trying. We may not be able to fix everything, or save everybody, but if we can make things a little better, that is a valiant goal. Recall the advice to meet people where they are, and start with small do-able changes. To quote some wisdom from the Talmud:

> *Do not be daunted by the enormity of the world's grief. Do justly, now. Love mercy, now. Walk humbly, now. You are not obligated to complete the work, but neither are you free to abandon it.*

All of the world's troubles probably have their roots stemming all the way back to Babel. Before Babel, so the story goes, everyone talked alike, and thought alike, and spoke the same language, and so getting along was easy.

One Friday night we were at Temple (we celebrate both our religious heritages, a melting pot of Jewish and Catholic faiths), and after reading the story of Babel again, the rabbi asked the congregation what we thought of this.

It took all of my self-control not to raise my hand and share my theory on the whole back-story to Babel. Mind you, it's just a theory.

I think maybe the Devil made a bet with God, saying that of course everyone got along, because they were all so similar and talked alike, walked alike, thought alike. But, what if you created differences? The Devil made a bet that things would fall apart quickly. God just could not believe this, having created all of these nice, beautiful, wonderful humans. He just could not picture them all behaving so badly, so he took the Devil up on his bet. And lost, on epic proportions.

As soon as the peoples were split into different groups, and spoke different languages, and thought differently, everything became much harder, and things literally went to hell in a handbag, as they say, and it has been that way ever since. That's my theory anyway.

Once humankind was splintered into different groups, factions, and cultures, it's no wonder that God would have had to make multiple visits and appear in different ways that would make the most sense for each local audience. It was no longer one-stop shopping. It's a construct of our little human minds to believe God only visited once or twice, and an inability to imagine God making multiple visits and taking many forms. God is God, and God should be able to come and go as He/She pleases.

One could ask, "Isn't it hard to believe in multiple visits from God, and multiple world religions, and isn't this pluralistic-theism?" And is that even a word? Religious pluralism is another term used. I simply believe all is possible. I'm not being asked to believe in anything less than what I grew up believing. I am simply open to believing in the mutual co-existence of multiple paths to God.

How many paths are there to God? There are as many paths to God as there are souls on earth.

Rumi

When you think about it, even across the major world religions, most of the differences are really relatively minor recent changes over the interpretation and implementation of religious beliefs, traditions, and rituals. The Devil really does dwell in the details! The majority of the differences though are really, at the 30,000-foot level, matters of subtle nuance, when you step back far enough.

For example, the difference between Christianity and Judaism rests on the question of whether Jesus was the Son of God, or just a good Jewish man, a great – albeit unconventional – teacher. So, whether we are awaiting the second or third coming of God might just be a detail. Who's counting? And, again, it is a reflection of our small human minds that we cannot grasp the idea of God taking multiple forms and making multiple visits.

Once Babel divided up human society, maybe God had to make many return visits, appearing in ways that made sense and resonated with the local cultures, indeed, meeting people where they were.

The most important message to draw from this is that there is a subtle but tremendous difference between merely having simple differences and being completely different. If you see another person as "an other," i.e., someone who is completely different from yourself, then it becomes possible to detach, lose empathy, and even carry out atrocities against them. This is the fundamental, underlying root cause to all the horrors in history, this loss of the ability to relate to and identify with others as fellow humans: the Holocaust, the Armenian genocide, all the genocides, in Nigeria and elsewhere, slavery, racism, xenophobia, the refugee crises, the struggle for human rights and dignity everywhere.

If we are able to recognize that all these differences (skin color, language, religion, etc.) are just minor differences, and that we are not all that different, then perhaps there still remains some hope, the possibility for finding common ground.

I found some very inspiring philosophical wisdom on this topic in a most unexpected place, at the Peeps & Company® store just outside D.C.

Inside we're all the same®

Peeps® T-shirt

There are elements from all religions worth looking at with an eye to possibly incorporating into your life what makes sense to you. Truly, just let love be your God.

One thing in the Buddhist tradition that has confused me for years is its emphasis on avoiding attachment, to things or even other people. Attachment brings suffering, therefore if you're not attached, you can't suffer, I suppose the thinking might go. Or, maybe we should only be attached to what is godly, and not earthly.

But having appetites and desires, and forming attachments all seem to me some of the very most fundamental parts of being human. We have physical appetites, hunger, for pleasure, food, sex, human contact. We have longings, desires, dreams, aims, goals, and aspirations. We have the ability to experience and express deep feelings, spanning the full, complex multi-dimensional range of human emotion, from great joy to deep sorrow, and everything up, down, left, right, and in-between. Even Jesus wept.

We are willing to go out on the field, and go all in, playing in this game of life. I would argue that all of these attributes, traits, emotions, desires, and appetites making up who we are as individuals – also essentially define what it is to be human.

All the experiences one has – good, bad, or indifferent, all the wins and losses along the way – expand one's ability to relate to others. The more we experience of this human world of loving, losing, winning, getting hurt, and finding joy, all of it makes us more well-versed in relating to others' human experiences, and so makes us better able to empathize with others. You've walked in their shoes. You've been there, or, as they say in Italian (according to *Eat Pray Love*, anyway):

L'ho provato sulla mia pelle.

Which translates roughly to:

I have experienced that on my own skin.

To visualize being in someone else's shoes, or skin, we have to drop any sense of entitlement due to birthright, and truly imagine that we could have born anywhere, under any set of circumstances ourselves. I call this the Deli Counter Theory. As the stork goes about delivering souls and/or babies, the stork just delivers them in the order their numbers come up, like at the deli counter. Same thing on the other end. Try to imagine that you could have been born, delivered anywhere.

> *There but for the grace of God go I.*
>
> John Bradford
> English preacher, 1510-1555

Maybe there is a more fundamental question in all of this. Maybe the question is this:

Are we human or divine?

And maybe the answer is yes, both.

Many, perhaps most, of the major world religions, at their core, share a common aim, to re-connect ourselves, our humanity, with what is constant, perfect, unchanging, and divine.

Even in yoga, at the end of each practice we say "Namasté," which literally translates to:

The light (divine) in me honors the light in you.

Brenda Ueland, perhaps the greatest writing teacher ever, offered up that the best thing we can do to love someone is to "see and believe" in the "god and poet" in them (Ueland, 1938).

What one comes to realize is that the world is full of paradoxes, and life is about co-existing with them, all the possibilities, simultaneously.

We are divine. We are human.
We are physical. We are spiritual.
We are feminine. We are masculine.
We are children. We are grown-ups.
We seek to belong. We seek to individuate.

And we are all both, all of these, all at the same time, a living contradiction, a study in contrasts, the ultimate paradox.

In the book, *My Stroke of Insight*, the author, Jill Bolte Taylor – a brain scientist – recounts her experience as she herself had a stroke, which affected the left side of her brain. During her recovery, as she was more reliant on the right side, and in fact processing the world predominantly through her right brain, she describes having an overwhelming sense of oneness with the universe. And as her left brain (the intellectual, scientific, analytical side) recovered, she feared and even grieved losing this primal sense. The crazy part is that we all have this right brain way of thinking available inside of us, if we can only tune into it, and mute the left brain chatter. Studies using MRI scans have shown that those in deep prayer or meditative thought, such as nuns and Tibetan monks, have reduced activity in the left brain and enhanced activity in the right brain.

So, the cure to everything – conflict resolution, world peace, happiness – all resides within us right now; latent, untapped potential, ready to burst forth.

We are meant to be both human and divine, children and grown-ups, belonging and individuals. And as I explored in my first book, both naked and weighted. If we take the words division and unity and combine them, you get divinity, the essence of being both at the same time.

I was struck by a particular letter to the editor I saw one day in *The Boston Globe*, back in 2006, that was inspired by the passing of the well-known peace activist, Reverend William Sloane Coffin. This letter actually sparked a lot of the thinking that ultimately led me to write this book, and so I have come full circle. This is where I began.

My thesis advisor, the late Richard M. Sillitto, often finished his lectures on the paradoxes of quantum mechanics with the quote: 'The test of a first-class intelligence is the ability to hold two opposed ideas in mind at the same time and still retain the ability to function.'

The quotation is from F. Scott Fitzgerald, who continues, 'One should, for example, be able to see that things are hopeless and yet be determined to make them otherwise.'

It was while reading James Carroll's remembrance of William Sloane Coffin (op-ed April 24) that I remembered where I had heard that thought again as recently as last week. National Public Radio broadcast an excerpt of an interview in which the Rev. Coffin said,

'If your heart's full of hope, you can be persistent when you can't be optimistic. You can keep the faith despite the evidence, knowing that only in so doing has the evidence any chance of changing. So, while I am not optimistic, I am always hopeful.'

A nice juxtaposition. In spite of our yearning for simple answers, we find in literature, in physics, in social justice, and, it seems, in life itself, that the acknowledgment and even the celebration of paradox and ambiguity can be paradoxically empowering."

Eric C. Kintner

I have carried this newspaper clipping with me in my back pocket for over a decade now, pulling it out whenever I needed some inspiration, to not give up, to try to make things better, to be both human and divine. If I could not always be optimistic, try as I might, I have always tried to remain hopeful.

Epilogue

It's funny, all the far-reaching, random interconnections we have, our shared points of light, and what seeds might be sown as a result; how a letter to the editor could serve as the point of inspiration for the rest of this book. I must confess, I didn't know of Reverend Sloane Coffin before I read this letter, but am ever grateful to Eric C. Kintner, and chance, for introducing me to his work, his letter to the editor like a message in a bottle thrown to the sea.

We are all so unbelievably fragile. We're all broken. This reminds me of the Japanese art form of broken objects, called Kintsugi, in which the jagged edges of pottery are healed with gold or other precious metals, and made whole again, lacquered to become a thing of beauty.

Shortly after losing my mom, I was at a Beantown Rugby reunion, and there was K.O. again, our wonderful, wise first captain, again sharing her new words of wisdom: "Be gentle with yourself." Wise words for us all.

Rose

Post Script

I did a crazy thing, a really crazy thing. I took a month off work to finish this book. I stayed at home, and went to my writing desk each morning, leaving it only to trot downstairs for lunch and tune into the news, and go for a walk. At the end of the month, on that last Friday, I hit "Save."

That was Friday the 28th of February, 2020.

Pre-pandemic, before the whole world changed. I saw it coming. As the CDC said, it was not a matter of if, but when it would arrive here. As I watched the news, I held out hope against hope that leaders would act and stave off the virus.

But, here we are now, and it is into this world, in the midst of a global pandemic, that this book on happiness comes out. The irony is not lost on me. All my messages about the importance of relationships and the pain of loneliness now stand in stark relief against the current landscape of isolation and social distancing. But, perhaps these messages of hope and happiness ring just as true and are needed just as much, if not more so now than ever before, and that is my hope for you, the reader.

In my defense, there was no way I could have known the timing would work out this way. It's not as if I wrote this thing overnight. I started this book years ago, way before anyone could have seen this coming. It was around 2006 that I started collecting the first random thoughts and articles, the flotsam and jetsam in the notebook in my back pocket. The first hand-written manuscript was drafted in 2014, and typed up in 2019. It turns out that I put out books at about the same frequency as the cicadas return. I'd be remiss not to mention the song, "It's Time," by Imagine Dragons, which helped me get through some dark times, served as my anthem for a while, and helped propel me forward to put pencil to paper and write again.

Over the past several weeks, I've often been reminded of the saying by New York City Fire Chaplain, Father Mychal Judge:

Want to make God laugh?
Tell Him what you're doing tomorrow.

This is made all the more poignant given that he was on the scene on 9/11, and the first recorded fatality that day (Hagerty, 2011; Jacobs, 2001).

Anyone who says they could never have imagined a pandemic need only to read more history and fiction, though. As a Geologist, I am used to looking out over much longer timelines of thousands and millions of years. There will be more meteorite impacts, volcanic eruptions, earthquakes, and floods. We just don't know when. Again, there is an infinite difference between the impossible and the improbable.

I've resisted the urge to go back and edit every page to reflect our new reality. It's too much. Instead, this stands as is; or as it was, like a fly caught in amber, or a fossil seashell preserved in stone. And now the very words I write here, too, shall stand as a time capsule, a snapshot in time.

So much loss, so much suffering, and so much hardship. I wonder what we will have learned through this. About ourselves. About each other. Did we learn anything about what we really need, about what really matters? Did we take time to slow down and reconnect?

I learned that both my mom and dad had always been right, to be prepared for hard times. They always emphasized the necessities: food, clothing, and shelter. Everything else is a luxury. They grew up in the shadow of the Depression. Because of them, I could always imagine a time such as these. Reading books helped, too, both fiction, such as *All the Light We Cannot See*, by Anthony Doerr, *The Weight of Ink*, by Rachel Kadish; and *A Gentleman in Moscow*, by Amor Towles; and biographies, such as *Long Walk to Freedom*, by Nelson Mandela, and the Louis Zamperini story, *Unbroken*, as told by Laura Hillenbrand. How many parents now are trying to reassure their children every night that everything is going to be alright? Saying it, even when they have no idea if that's true.

The doctors and scientists were right about the coronavirus. Maybe it's time for people to listen to the scientists about other things, too, like climate change.

I know what I would be doing if I still worked at the hospital cafeteria in Dayton: brewing coffee!

I wish I could bring a flower or plant to every patient's room. I wish there could be calming, familiar music playing for them, and friends and family by their bedside. I have renewed appreciation for how fortunate I was to be with Angie and my mom in their final days, knowing how many families now have been deprived of this last good bye, unable to visit their loved ones in nursing homes and hospitals.

My heart is filled with gratitude for the nurses and doctors, and all the healthcare workers, fighting to save lives, as well as all the front-line workers sustaining lives: grocery stores, pharmacies, delivery services, bus drivers, restaurants, food supply, meat packing plants, etc. I am more grateful now than ever before for food and all the people who help bring it to store shelves. My mom worked at a grocery store for a while, and later in a factory, packaging shredded wheat cereal. She would have been on the front line. And Angie would have been so vulnerable.

The pandemic has revealed social and economic disparities, as the risk of continued function during this pandemic has been shifted disproportionately to these front-line workers. These positions are largely blue collar, low-paying, and filled predominantly by minorities, underscoring and magnifying the economic inequalities in society.

In addition to the health risk, the pandemic has inflicted tremendous financial hardships for the millions of workers now unemployed and small businesses shuttered. The crisis has also highlighted the need for a living wage, universal access to healthcare, and character in our public leaders. Instead there was only denial and delay. So many failures in leadership at so many levels, with only a few bright spots along the way, such as Massachusetts Governor Charlie Baker, New York Governor Andrew Cuomo, and Dr. Anthony Fauci.

Otherwise, we are all sitting and waiting and watching, wondering when it will be our turn to find out if we are going to get the coronavirus, and when we do, if it will be a mild or more severe case. If you start experiencing symptoms, of course, call your doctor. Medical experts are also now suggesting that patients lie on their stomach or on their side, to help prevent compressing the smallest blood vessels in the air sacs in the lungs (Shastri and Boulton, 2020). I first saw this advice from a most unexpected source thanks to the Twitterverse. J. K. Rowling shared a tweet by Dr. Safaraz Munshi at Queen's Hospital in England, demonstrating this technique and some breathing exercises in a YouTube video (Bensadoun, 2020; Munshi, 2020). Once again, I am not a doctor, but this seems like good advice.

I've been keeping up with my morning exercise routine (wall angels, overhead presses, squats, etc.). In some small ways we might be healthier than ever before, with less driving, less commuting stress, and so many people out walking and jogging, and children playing outside. We've been finding new places to walk within our urban environment, and the woods west of town have been filled with people. As Meghan pointed out in a margin note in Chapter 4, "It seems there's a natural pull to the woods for comfort and reset; almost as if it's primal." And, again, a big thank you to Meghan Regan-Loomis for her editorial wisdom and for pushing me to dig a little deeper in places, and truly helping to make this a better work.

We've been watching nature right outside our window, as the robins returned to nest in our rhododendron, laying their eggs, chicks hatching, and now on the verge of fledging. And fledge they did.

We've been cooking and baking. Enjoying my mom's pizza, thanks to the frozen crusts we had in the freezer. We had a package of dates on hand, and used my mom's old recipe to make date bars. I'm sharing the recipe here now (turn the page) so it might bring you some comfort and cheer too.

I've sought and found comfort in the smallest of things. My softest fleece. Lavender soap. The company of friends, albeit virtually. Putting my hands together. Putting my hands together in prayer each night still. "God bless..." God bless everyone. God help us all.

Music has been a salve for the soul, too. A couple of very different songs have resonated with me through these past many days: "Pale Grass Blue," by Enya, and "The Ghost in You," by Psychedelic Furs. They just struck a chord with me, these songs of sun and rain, angels and butterflies, falling and flying away.

Old favorites have also been a source of comfort: "Let It Be," "In the Sun," and "Everybody Lost Somebody," this last one written by Jack Antonoff of the Bleachers, about the loss of his sister. I related to this song right away, for obvious reasons, but now it carries so much more weight in the current landscape.

We don't know how this story ends. What we do know is that no one will be untouched by this pandemic.

Add to this global health crisis, the unfolding human rights tragedy and public outcry over the death of George Floyd, coming on the heels of the shootings of Breonna Taylor in March, and Ahmaud Arbery in February, and so many more before them. George Floyd's murder was captured on video, which went viral, the shocking footage of the policeman pressing his knee into George's neck, even as he pleaded for his life, and repeatedly told the police officers that he couldn't breathe. Until he gave his last breath. Isn't the suffering and loss of even one Black man's or woman's life one too many?

I can't pretend to know the African-American experience, all the day-to-day indignities, the legacy of slavery, and the enduring opportunity inequalities. I can only imagine, with compassion, humility, and empathy, and a heart held open.

How does change happen? When is enough, enough? Perhaps we have reached the 'tipping point' to use Malcolm Gladwell's term, akin to the night in June of 1969 when a bunch of drag queens resisted arrest and riots erupted after yet another police raid at the Stonewall Inn in New York City, sparking the gay rights movement. My hope is that this is more than a moment, and truly a movement, for Black Lives Matter.

There was the image of George Floyd's six-year old daughter, Gianna, spinning in the crowd, surrounded by the signs and murals honoring her father. So young, smiling, and so innocent, she says: "Daddy changed the world." And it breaks my heart. I hope he does.

In a world that is on fire, we need unity and divinity now more so than ever before. My hope is that we can come together, and the depths of these tragedies may be transcended by all that is good in the world, and that all the simplest and smallest acts of kindness can help shine a light through these difficult times.

Be gentle with yourself.
Be gentle with each other.

Date Bars

Ingredients:
Filling:
1 lb dates (about 18 large Medjool), chopped
¼ cup sugar
Crust:
¾ cup butter
1 cup brown sugar
1 ¾ cups flour
½ tsp salt
½ tsp baking soda
1 ½ cups oats
Decoration:
Powdered sugar

Take butter out earlier in the day to let it soften.

Put the chopped dates and ¼ cup sugar in a saucepan, and add 1 ½ cups water. Stir over low heat until thickened, about 10 minutes. Set aside to cool.

Preheat oven to 400° F.

Grease a 13 x 9 x 2 pan or casserole dish.

Cream together the brown sugar and butter. My mom's original recipe called for ¼ cup shortening and

½ cup butter, but we usually use all butter (1½ sticks), and sometimes cut it down by a little.

Mix together the other dry ingredients for the crust: flour, salt, and baking soda. My mom's original recipe called for a full teaspoon of salt, but we've backed it down to ½ or even just ¼ teaspoon. Add the dry ingredients to the butter-brown sugar mixture, and blend in together, using a fork. Mix in the quick-cooking oats (uncooked oatmeal).

Sprinkle about half the crust mixture in the pan, and gently but firmly press into place.

Once the date filling has cooled, spread it evenly across the bottom crust with a spoon. Sprinkle the remaining crust mixture over the top of the filling, and gently press into place.

Bake for 30 minutes, or until crust is light brown. Allow to cool. Sift powdered sugar over the top, cut into squares, and enjoy.

Serve with love.

References

Abbasi, Behnood, Masud Kimiagar, Khosro Sadeghniiat, Minoo M. Shirazi, Mehdi Hedayati, and Bahram Rashidkhani. 2012. The effect of magnesium supplementation on primary insomnia in elderly: A double-blind placebo-controlled clinical trial. *Journal of Research in Medical Sciences*. December 2012. 17(12):1161–1169.
https://www.ncbi.nlm.nih.gov/pmc/articles/PMC3703169/

Achor, Shawn. 2010. *The Happiness Advantage: How a Positive Brain Fuels Success in Work and Life*. New York: Currency, an imprint of Crown Publishing Group, a division of Penguin Random House LLC.

Ackerman, Joshua M., Christopher C. Nocera, and John A. Bargh. 2010. Incidental haptic sensations influence social judgments and decisions. *Science*. 25 June 2010. 328(5986):1712-1715.
http://science.sciencemag.org/content/328/5986/1712

Adams, Ryan. 2001. When the Stars Go Blue. On *Gold*. Lost Highway Records, Universal Music Group Nashville.

Aldrich, Daniel P. 2012. *Building Resilience: Social Capital in Post-Disaster Recovery*. Chicago: University of Chicago Press.

Aldrich, Daniel P. 2017. In disaster recovery, social networks matter more than bottled water and batteries. *The Conversation*. 13 Feb 2017.
https://theconversation.com/recovering-from-disasters-social-networks-matter-more-than-bottled-water-and-batteries-69611

Allen, Andrew P., and Andrew P. Smith. 2015. Chewing gum: Cognitive performance, mood, well-being, and associated physiology. *BioMed Research International*. 17 May 2015. Volume 2015.
https://doi.org/10.1155/2015/654806

Allis, Sam. 2010. His beat is the world's afflicted. *The Boston Globe*. 18 February 2010.
http://archive.boston.com/ae/tv/articles/2010/02/18/hbo_turns_camera_on_reporter/

Associated Press. 2017. Einstein's 'theory of happiness' nets $1.3M. *The Boston Globe*. 25 October 2017.

Aucoin, Don. 2006. Nice try: Public politeness, good news? There's a growing movement to get happy. *The Boston Globe*. 20 December 2006.

Arnold, Linda. 2019. 75-Year Harvard study: What makes us happy? *Associated Press*. 21 April 2019.
https://apnews.com/6dab1e79c34e4514af8d184d951f5733

Arthur, Joseph. 2000. In the Sun. On *Come to Where I'm From*. Real World Records.
https://youtu.be/uNF2cbW37mo

Bakalar, Nicholas. 2010. Happiness may come with age, study says. *The New York Times*. 31 May 2010.
https://www.nytimes.com/2010/06/01/health/research/01happy.html

Bao, Ying, Jiali Han, Frank B. Hu, Edward L. Giovannucci, Meir J. Stampfer, Walter C. Willett, and Charles S. Fuchs. 2013. Association of nut consumption with total and cause-specific mortality. *The New England Journal of Medicine*. 21 November 2013. Volume 369:2001-2011.
https://www.nejm.org/doi/full/10.1056/NEJMoa1307352

Baumeister, Roy F., and John Tierney. 2012. *Willpower: Rediscovering the Greatest Human Strength*. New York: Penguin Books.

Bender, Bryan. 2012. Training cadets for war and (inner) peace. *The Boston Globe*. 2 December 2012.

Bensadoun, Emerald. 2020. Coronavirus patients are being flipped onto their stomachs in the ICU – here's why. *Global News*. 8 April 2020.
https://globalnews.ca/news/6788251/breathing-technique-coronavirus/

Benson, Herbert, M.D. 1975. *The Relaxation Response*. New York: Avon Books, in arrangement with William Morrow and Company, Inc.

Berman, Marc G., Ethan Kross, Katherine M. Krpan, Mary K. Askren, Aleah Burson, Patricia J. Deldin, Stephen Kaplan, Lindsey Sherdell, Ian H. Gotlib, and John Jonides. 2012. Interaction with nature improves

cognition and affect for individuals with depression. *Journal of Affective Disorders*. November 2012. 140(3):300-305.
https://dx.doi.org/10.1016%2Fj.jad.2012.03.012

Bernstein, Emily E., Alexandre Heeren, and Richard J. McNally. 2017. Unpacking rumination and executive control: A network perspective. *Clinical Psychological Science*. 11 June 2017. 5(5):816-826.
https://doi.org/10.1177%2F2167702617702717

Bestbier, Lana, and Tim I. Williams. 2017. The immediate effects of deep pressure on young people with autism and severe intellectual difficulties: Demonstrating individual differences. *Occupational Therapy International*. 9 January 2017.
https://dx.doi.org/10.1155%2F2017%2F7534972

Beukeboom, C., D. Langeveld, and K. Tanja-Dijkstra. 2012. Stress-reducing effects of real and artificial nature in a hospital waiting room. *The Journal of Alternative and Complementary Medicine*. April 2012. 18(4):329-333.
https://doi.org/10.1089/acm.2011.0488

Blanchflower, David G., and Andrew Oswald. 2017. Do humans suffer a psychological low in midlife? Two approaches (with and without controls) in seven data sets. *National Bureau of Economic Research*. Working Paper No. 23724. August 2017.
http://www.nber.org/papers/w23724

Bleachers. 2014. I Wanna Get Better. On *I Wanna Get Better*. Sony/ATV Music Publishing LLC. https://youtu.be/o5osPtE7kXI

Bleachers. 2017. Everybody Lost Somebody. On *Gone Now*. RCA Records. https://youtu.be/khqRs0g3wvE

Boyle, Neil Bernard, Clare Lawton, and Louise Dye. 2017. The effects of magnesium supplementation on subjective anxiety and stress – A systematic review. *Nutrients*. 26 April 2017. 9(5):429.
https://doi.org/10.3390/nu9050429

Breines, Juliana G., and Serena Chen. 2012. Self-compassion increases self-improvement motivation. *Personality and Social Psychology Bulletin.* 29 May 2012.
https://doi.org/10.1177/0146167212445599

Brittle, Zach. 2015. Turn towards instead of away. *The Gottman Institute.* 1 April 2015.
https://www.gottman.com/blog/turn-toward-instead-of-away/

Brown, Alexander, and Joanna Lahey. 2014. Small victories: Creating intrinsic motivation in savings and debt reduction. *National Bureau of Economic Research. Working Paper 20125. May 2014.*
https://ssrn.com/abstract=2438546

Brown, Lillian. 2019. More secrets to Brady's success: Healing stones, mantras, and listening to Gisele. *The Boston Globe.* 12 February 2019.

Bruce, Liana DesHarnais, Joshua S. Wu, Stuart L. Lustig, Daniel W. Russell, and Douglas A. Nemecek. 2019. Loneliness in the United States: A 2018 National Panel Survey of demographic, structural, cognitive, and behavioral characteristics. *American Journal of Health Promotion.* 16 June 2019. 33(8):1123-1133.
https://doi.org/10.1177%2F0890117119856551

Burkett, J. P., E. Andari, Z. V. Johnson, D. C. Curry, F. B. M. de Waal, and L. J. Young. 2016. Oxytocin-dependent consolation behavior in rodents. *Science.* 22 January 2016. 351(6271):375-378.
https://doi.org/10.1126/science.aac4785

Burkus, David. 2017. Why you can focus in a coffee shop but not in your open office. *Harvard Business Review.* 18 October 2017.
https://hbr.org/2017/10/why-you-can-focus-in-a-coffee-shop-but-not-in-your-open-office

Cao, Kun, Jie Xiang, Yang-Ting Dong, Hui Song, Xiao-Xiao Zeng, Long-Yan Ran, Wei Hong, and Zhi-Zhong Guan. 2019. Exposure to fluoride aggravates the impairment in learning and memory and neuropathological lesions in mice carrying the APP/PS1 double-transgenic mutation. *Alzheimer's Research and Therapy.* 22 April 2019.
https://alzres.biomedcentral.com/articles/10.1186/s13195-019-0490-3

Carlson, Richard. 1997. *Don't Sweat the Small Stuff… and It's All Small Stuff: Simple Ways to Keep the Little Things from Taking Over Your Life.* New York: Hyperion.

Carmichael, Sarah Green. 2015. The research is clear: Long hours backfire for people and for companies. *Harvard Business Review.* 19 August 2015.

Carroll, James. 2006. A genius of a man, he believed in hope. *The Boston Globe.* 24 April 2006.

Chabris, Christopher F, Patrick R. Heck, Jaclyn Mandart, Daniel J. Benjamin, and Daniel J. Simons. 2019. No evidence that experiencing physical warmth promotes interpersonal warmth: Two failures to replicate Williams and Bargh (2008). *Social Psychology.* March 2019. 50(2):127-132.
https://doi.org/10.1027/1864-9335/a000361

Chen, Hsin-Yung, Hsiang Yang, Huang-Ju Chi, and Hsin-Ming Chen. 2012. Physiological effects of deep touch pressure on anxiety alleviation: The weighted blanket approach. *Journal of Medical and Biological Engineering.* 33(5):463-470.
http://www.jmbe.org.tw/files/1961/public/1961-5094-1-PB.pdf

Chen, Zhansheng, Kai-Tak Poon, and C. Nathan DeWall. 2014. When do socially accepted people feel ostracized? Physical pain triggers social pain. *Social Influence.* 19 June 2014. 10(1):68-76.
https://www.tandfonline.com/doi/abs/10.1080/15534510.2014.926290

Cigna and Ipsos. 2018. *Cigna U.S. Loneliness Index: Survey of 20,000 Americans Examining Behaviors Driving Loneliness in the United States.*
https://www.cigna.com/about-us/newsroom/studies-and-reports/combatting-loneliness/

Cigna. 2020. *Loneliness and the Workplace: 2020 U.S. Report.*
https://www.cigna.com/about-us/newsroom/studies-and-reports/combatting-loneliness/

Clark, Nancy F. 2014. Act now to shrink the confidence gap. *ForbesWoman.* 28 April 2014.

http://www.forbes.com/sites/womensmedia/2014/04/28/act-now-to-shrink-the-confidence-gap/

Coffin, William Sloane. 2004. *Credo*. Louisville, Kentucky: Westminster John Knox Press.

Covey, Stephen R. 1989. *The Seven Habits of Effective People*. New York: Free Press.

Cracknell, Deborah, Matthew P. White, Sabine Pahl, Wallace J. Nichols, and Michael H. Depledge, 2015. Marine biota and psychological well-being: A preliminary examination of dose-response effects in an aquarium setting. *Journal of Environment and Behavior*. Online 28 July 2015. December 2016. 48(10):1242-1269.
https://doi.org/10.1177%2F0013916515597512

Cuciureanu, Magdalena D., and Robert Vink. 2011. Magnesium and stress. *Magnesium in the Central Nervous System*, edited by Robert Vink and Mihai Nechifor. Adelaide, South Australia: University of Adelaide Press.
https://www.ncbi.nlm.nih.gov/books/NBK507250/
https://doi.org/10.1017/UPO9780987073051

Cuddy, Amy. 2015. *Presence: Bringing Your Boldest Self to Your Biggest Challenges*. New York: Little, Brown, and Company.

Cuddy, Amy J. C., S. Jack Schultz, and Nathan E. Fosse. 2018. P-curving a more comprehensive body of research on postural feedback reveals clear evidential value for power-posing effects: Reply to Simmon and Simmonsohn (2017). *Psychological Science*. 2 March 2018.
https://doi.org/10.1177%2F0956797617746749

Damisch, Lysann, Barbara Stoberock, and Thomas Mussweiler. 2010. Keep your fingers crossed! How superstitions improve performance. *Psychological Science*. 28 May 2010. 21(7):1014-1020.
https://doi.org/10.1177%2F0956797610372631

Darley, J. M., and C. D. Batson. 1973. From Jerusalem to Jericho: A study of situational variables in helping behavior. *Journal of Personality and Social Psychology*. Volume 27:100-108.

Davis, Nicole. 2019. Try this: 17 Exercises to relieve upper back pain, neck pain, and more. *Healthline*. 25 March 2019.
https://www.healthline.com/health/fitness-exercise/upper-back-pain-exercises

de Groot, Jasper H. B., Monique A. M. Smeets, and Gün R. Semin. 2015. Rapid stress system drives chemical transfer of fear from sender to receiver. *PLoS ONE*. 27 February 2015.
https://doi.org/10.1371/journal.pone.0118211

de Silva, Prasanna. 2018. Do patterns of synaptic pruning underlie psychoses, autism, and ADHD? *BJPsych Adv*. May 2018.
https://www.researchgate.net/publication/324768290_Do_patterns_of_s ynaptic_pruning_underlie_pychoses_autism_and_ADHD

DeWall, C. Nathan, Geoff MacDonald, Gregory D. Webster, Carrie L. Masten, Roy F. Baumeister, Caitlin Powell, David Combs, David R. Schurtz, Tyler F. Stillman, Dianne M. Tice, and Naomi I. Eisenberger. 2010. Acetaminophen reduces social pain: Behavioral and neural evidence. *Psychological Science*. 14 June 2010. 21(7):931-937.
https://doi.org/10.1177%2F0956797610374741

Doerr, Anthony. 2014. *All the Light We Cannot See*. New York: Scribner.

Downing, Michael. 2005. *Spring Forward: The Annual Madness of Daylight Saving Time*. Washington, D.C.: Shoemaker and Hoard.
Duhigg, Charles. 2012. *The Power of Habit*. New York: Random House.

Dusek, J. A., H. H. Otu, A. L. Wohlhueter, M. Bhasin, L. F. Zerbini, M. G. Joseph, H. Benson, and T. A. Libermann. 2008. Genomic counter-stress changes induced by the relaxation response. *PLoS One*. July 2008. 3(7):e2576.
https://doi.org/10.1371/journal.pone.0002576

Einstein, Albert. 1922. Unpublished note.

Eisenberger, Naomi I., Matthew D. Lieberman, and Kipling D. Williams. 2003. Does rejection hurt? An fMRI study of social exclusion. *Science*. 10 October 2013. 302(5643):290-292.
https://doi.org/10.1126/science.1089134

Eliot, George. 1872. *Middlemarch: A Study of Provincial Life*.

Elsesser, Kim. 2018. Power posing is back: Amy Cuddy successfully refutes criticism. *Forbes*. 3 April 2018.

Emswiler, Tom. 2014. Time to leave. *The Boston Globe*. 5 October 2014.

English, Bella. 2015. How to bounce back. *The Boston Globe*. 1 September 2015.

Enya. 2015. Pale Grass Blue. On *Dark Sky Island*. Sony/ATV Music Publishing Limited.
http://enya.sk/music/dark-sky-island/pale-grass-blue/

Epel, Elissa S., Bruce McEwen, Teresa Seeman, Karen Matthews, Grace Castellazzo, Kelly D. Brownell, Jennifer Bell, and Jeannette R. Ickovics. 2000. Stress and body shape: Stress-induced cortisol secretion is consistently greater among women with central fat. *Psychosomatic Medicine*. September-October 2000. 62(5):623-632.
https://journals.lww.com/psychosomaticmedicine/Abstract/2000/09000/ Stress_and_Body_Shape__Stress_Induced_Cortisol.5.aspx

Etcoff, Nancy. Driving ourselves happy. Talk given at HUBWeek Women in Medicine Series. 28 October 2015.

Falk, Emily B., Matthew Brook O'Donnell, Christopher N. Cascio, Francis Tinney, Yoona Kang, Matthew D. Lieberman, Shelley E. Taylor, Lawrence An, Kenneth Resnicow, and Victor J. Strecher. 2015. Self-affirmation alters the brain response to health messages and subsequent behavior change. *Proceedings of the National Academy of Science of the United States*. 2 Feb 2015.

Faruque, Samir, Janice Tong, Vuk Lacmanovic, Christiana Agbonghae, Dulce M. Minaya, and Krzysztof Czaja. 2020. The dose makes the poison: Sugar and obesity in the United States – a review. *Polish Journal of Food and Nutrition Sciences*. 14 January 2020. 69(3):219-233.
https://doi.org/10.31883/pjfns/110735

Fitzgerald, F. Scott. 1936. The Crack-Up. *Esquire*. 1 February 1936.

Flora Cash. 2018. You're Somebody Else (Official Video). *YouTube*. 4 November 2018. https://youtu.be/AzjMmwki1Fs

Flora Cash. 2019. Missing Home (Official Video). *YouTube*. 5 September 2019. https://youtu.be/PAP2sv8O-OM

Florence + The Machine. 2018. Hunger (Official Video). *YouTube*. 3 May 2018. https://youtu.be/5GHXEGz3PJg

Ford, Brett Q., Amanda J. Shallcross, Iris B. Mauss, Victoria A. Floerke, and June Gruber. 2014. Desperately seeking happiness: Valuing happiness is associated with symptoms and diagnosis of depression. *Journal of Social and Clinical Psychology*. 1 December 2014. 33(10):890-905. https://dx.doi.org/10.1521%2Fjscp.2014.33.10.890

Fowler, James H., and Nicholas A. Christakis. 2008. Dynamic spread of happiness in a large social network: Longitudinal analysis over 20 years in the Framingham Heart Study. *British Medical Journal*. 5 December 2008. 337:a2338.
https://doi.org/10.1136/bmj.a2338

Fredrickson, Barbara L., and Marcial F. Losada. 2005. Positive affect and the complex dynamics of human flourishing. *American Psychology*. October 2005. 60(7):678-686.
https://dx.doi.org/10.1037%2F0003-066X.60.7.678

Friedman, Harris L., and Nicholas J. L. Brown. 2018. Implications of debunking the "Critical Positivity Ratio" for humanistic psychology: Introduction to special issue. *Journal of Humanistic Psychology*. 29 March 2018. 58(3):239-261.
https://doi.org/10.1177%2F0022167818762227

Fulton, Cindy. 2014. *The Impact of Real and Artificial Plants on the Patient Experience in the Hospital Setting*. Capstone Project, School of Physician Assistant Studies, Pacific University.
https://commons.pacificu.edu/pa/502/

Gilbert, Daniel. 2006. *Stumbling on Happiness*. New York: Vintage Books, a division of Random House, Inc.

Gilbert, Elizabeth. 2006. *Eat Pray Love: One Woman's Search for Everything Across Italy, India, and Thailand.* New York: Viking Penguin.

Glaveski, Steve. 2017. The case for the 6-hour workday. *Harvard Business Review.* 11 December 2018.

Gottman, John M. 1999. *The Marriage Clinic: A Scientifically Based Marital Therapy.* New York: W. W. Norton and Company.

Gottman, John Mordechai, and Nan Silver. 1999. *The Seven Principles for Making Marriage Work.* New York: Harmony Books, an imprint of the Crown Publishing Group, a division of Random House LLC, a Penguin Random House Company.

Graham, Brendan. 2002. You Raise Me Up (lyrics).

Grandin, Temple. 1995. *Thinking in Pictures, Expanded Edition: My Life with Autism.* New York: Vintage Books, a division of Random House.

Grassman, Deborah. 2015. Help PTSD sufferers heal from 'soul injury'. *The Boston Globe.* 22 June 2015.

Green, Rachel, and Wendy Rhodes. 2019. Autism and ADHD: Signs, treatments, and therapies. *Weighted Blanket Guides.* 18 December 2019. https://www.weightedblanketguides.com/benefits-autism-adhd/

Hagerty, Barbara Bradley. 2011. Memories of September 11's first recorded casualty endure. *National Public Radio.* 5 September 2011. https://www.npr.org/2011/09/05/140154885/memories-of-sept-11s-first-casualty-burn-bright

Hamedani, MarYam G., Hazel Rose Markus, and Alyssa S. Fu. 2013. In the land of the free, interdependent action undermines motivation. *Psychological Science.* 9 January 2013. 24(2):189-196. https://web.stanford.edu/~hazelm/publications/2013%20Hamedani%20Markus%20Fu%20In%20the%20Land%20of%20the%20Free,%20Interdependent%20Action%20Undermines%20Motivation.pdf

Hammond, Claudia. 2019. Does reading fiction make us better people? *BBC.* 2 June 2019.

Hale, Gill. 2002. *The Practical Encyclopedia of Feng Shui*. London: Hermes House.

Hamer, Mark, and G. David Batty. 2019. Association of body mass index and waist-to-hip ratio with brain structure. *Neurology*. 5 February 2019. 92(6):594-600.

Hannon, Kerry. 2014. Are women too timid when they job search? *Forbes*. 11 September 2014.
http://www.forbes.com/sites/nextavenue/2014/09/11/are-women-too-timid-when-they-job-search/

Harada, Hiroki, Hideki Kashiwadani, Yuichi Kanmura, and Tomoyuki Kuwaki. 2018. Linalool odor-induced anxiolytic effects in mice. *Frontiers in Behavioral Neuroscience*. 23 October 2018. Volume 12, Article 241.
https://dx.doi.org/10.3389%2Ffnbeh.2018.00241

Hansen, George R., and Jon Streltzer. 2005. The psychology of pain. *Emergency Medicine Clinics of North America*. May 2005. 23(2):339-348.
https://doi.org/10.1016/j.emc.2004.12.005

Hartnett, Kevin. 2016. Console like a vole. *The Boston Globe*. 7 February 2016.

Hayward, H'Sien. 2013. *Post-Traumatic Growth and Disability: On Happiness, Positivity, and Meaning*. Doctoral Dissertation, Harvard University.
https://dash.harvard.edu/handle/1/11156671

Heid, Markham. 2017. Trying too hard to be happy can make you feel like crap. *Vice*. 21 November 2017.
https://www.vice.com/en_us/article/bj7b9v/trying-to-be-happy

Hicks, Donna. 2011. *Dignity: The Essential Role It Plays in Resolving Conflict*. New Haven, Connecticut: Yale University Press.

Hillenbrand, Laura. 2010. *Unbroken: A World War II Story of Survival, Resilience, and Redemption*. New York: Random House.

Hoile, Penny. 2019. Create a culture of working less hours and you'll boost productivity: Here's why. *Sage*. 30 September 2019.
https://www.sagepeople.com/about-us/news-hub/creating-culture-working-less-boost-productivity/

Holt-Lunstad, Juliane, Timothy B. Smith, Mark Baker, Tyler Harris, and David Stephenson. 2015. Loneliness and social isolation as risk factors for mortality: A meta-analytical review. *Perspectives on Psychological Science*. 11 March 2015. 10(2):227-237.
https://doi.org/10.1177/1745691614568352

Howley, Elaine K. 2019. Is there a connection between aluminum and Alzheimer's disease? *U.S. News and World Report*. 12 June 2019.
https://health.usnews.com/conditions/alzheimers/articles/is-there-a-connection-between-aluminum-and-alzheimers-disease

Hullinger, Jessica. 2015. The science of why we fidget while we work. *Fast Company*. 24 March 2015.
https://www.fastcompany.com/3044026/the-science-of-why-we-fidget-while-we-work

Huston, Therese. 2017. Men can be so hormonal. *The New York Times*. 24 June 2017.
https://www.nytimes.com/2017/06/24/opinion/sunday/men-testosterone-hormones.html

Iaccarino, Hannah F., Annabelle C. Singer, Anthony J. Martorell, Andrii Rudenko, Fan Gao, Tyler Z. Gillingham, Hansruedi Mathys, Jinsoo Seo, Oleg Kritskiy, Fatema Abdurrob, Chinnakkaruppan Adaikkan, Rebecca G. Canter, Richard Rueda, Emery N. Brown, Edward S. Boyden, and Li-Huei Tsai. 2016. Gamma frequency entrainment attenuates amyloid load and modifies microglia. *Nature*. 7 December 2016. 540(7632):230-235.
https://www.ncbi.nlm.nih.gov/pmc/articles/PMC5656389/

Imagine Dragons. 2012. It's Time. On *Night Visions*. Universal Music Publishing Group.

Ingraham, Christopher. 2017. Under 50? You still haven't hit rock bottom, happiness-wise. *The Washington Post*. 24 August 2017.

https://www.washingtonpost.com/news/wonk/wp/2017/08/24/under-50-you-still-havent-hit-rock-bottom-happiness-wise/?utm_term=.2fba287aef13

Interlandi, Jeneen. The brain's empathy gap: Can mapping neural pathways help us make friends with our enemies? *New York Times.* 19 March 2015.
https://www.nytimes.com/2015/03/22/magazine/the-brains-empathy-gap.html

Jacobs, Jeff. 2001. Look no further for real heroes. *Hartford Courant.* 17 September 2001.
https://www.courant.com/news/connecticut/hc-xpm-2001-09-17-0109170588-story.html

Jacobs, Rachel H., Lisanne M. Jenkins, Laura B. Gabriel, Alyssa Barba, Kelly A. Ryan, Sara L. Weisenbach, Alvaro Verges, Amanda M. Baker, Amy T. Peters, Natania A. Crane, Ian H. Gotlib, Jon-Kar Zubieta, K. Luan Phan, Scott A. Langenecker, and Robert C. Welsh. 2014. Increased coupling of intrinsic networks in remitted depressed youth predicts rumination and cognitive control. *PLoS ONE.* 27 August 2014. 9(8):1-11.
https://doi.org/10.1371/journal.pone.0104366

Jacobsen, Jörn-Henrik, Johannes Stelzer, Thomas Hans Fritz, Gael Chételat, Renaud La Joie, and Robert Turner. 2015. Why musical memory can be preserved in advanced Alzheimer's disease. *Brain.* 3 June 2015. 138(8):2438-2450.
https://doi.org/10.1093/brain/awv135

James, Henry. 1881. *The Portrait of a Lady.* Boston: Houghton Mifflin.

James, William. 1901-1902. *The Varieties of Religious Experience: A Study in Human Nature.* The Gifford Lectures on Natural Religion Delivered at Edinburgh in 1901-1902. Edited and Annotated for the World Wide Web by LeRoy L. Miller.
https://www.nwarkaa.org/var.pdf

Jebb, Andrew T., Louis Tay, Ed Diener, and Shigehiro Oishi. 2018. Happiness, income satiation, and turning points around the world. *Nature Human Behaviour.* 8 January 2018. 2(1):33-38.

https://www.researchgate.net/deref/https%3A%2F%2Fwww.nature.com%2Farticles%2Fs41562-017-0277-0

Joel, Billy. 1977. Just The Way You Are. On *The Stranger*. A & R Recording. 1977.

Johnson, Carolyn Y. 2008. New reason to be happy: It may go a long way. *The Boston Globe*. 5 December 2008.

Johnson, Carolyn Y. 2014. McLean team explores mechanism for erasing painful memories. *The Boston Globe*. 1 September 2014.

Johnson, Dan R. 2012. Transportation into a story increases empathy, prosocial behavior, and perceptual bias toward fearful expressions. *Personality and Individual Differences*. January 2012. 52(2):150-155. https://doi.org/10.1016/j.paid.2011.10.005

Johnston, Katie. 2014. Workers happier with members of same gender, study finds. *The Boston Globe*. October 6, 2014. http://www.bostonglobe.com/business/2014/10/06/gender-diversity-increases-productivity-decreases-happiness/dOiNvWK9tj8qJyrKVGp3uI/story.html

Jones, Marggie, Barry McDermott, Bárbara Luz Oliveira, Aoife O'Brien, Declan Coogan, Mark Lang, Niamh Moriarty, Eilis Dowd, Leo Quinlan, Brian McGinley, Eoghan Dunne, David Newell, Emily Porter, Muhammad Adnan Elahi, Martin O'Halloran, and Atif Shazad. 2019. Gamma band light stimulation in human case studies: Groundwork for potential Alzheimer's disease treatment. *Journal of Alzheimer's Disease*. 2 July 2019. 70(1):171-185. https://www.ncbi.nlm.nih.gov/pmc/articles/PMC6700637/

Kadish, Rachel. 2017. *The Weight of Ink*. Boston: Houghton Mifflin.

Kahneman, Daniel, and Alan B. Krueger. 2006. Developments in the Measurement of Subjective Well-Being. *Journal of Economic Perspective*. Winter 2006. 20(1):3-24. https://www.aeaweb.org/articles?id=10.1257/089533006776526030

Karlesky, Michael, and Katherine Isbister. 2014. Designing for the physical margins of digital workspaces: Fidget widgets in support of productivity and creativity. *Conference Proceedings of the 8th International Conference on Tangible, Embedded and Embodied Interaction.* February 2014. https://doi.org/10.1145/2540930.2559982

Kay, Katty, and Claire Shipman. 2014. The confidence gap. *The Atlantic.* May 2014. http://www.theatlantic.com/features/archive/2014/04/the-confidence-gap/359815/

Kearns, Cristin E., Laura A. Schmidt, and Stanton A. Glantz. 2016. Sugar industry and coronary heart disease research: A historical analysis of internal industry documents. *JAMA Internal Medicine.* November 2016. 176(11):1680-1685. doi:10.1001/jamainternmed.2016.5394

Kelly, Jack. 2020. Finland Prime Minister's aspirational goal of a six-hour, four-day workweek: Will it ever happen? *Forbes.* 8 January 2020. https://www.forbes.com/sites/jackkelly/2020/01/08/finlands-prime-ministers-aspirational-goal-of-a-six-hour-four-day-workweek-will-this-ever-happen/#51d101f03638

Kintner, Eric C. 2006. Letter to Editor. *The Boston Globe.* 29 April 2006.

Knapton, Sarah. 2015. Fish tanks lower blood pressure and heart rate. *The Telegraph.* 30 July 2015. https://www.telegraph.co.uk/news/science/science-news/11770965/Fish-tanks-lower-blood-pressure-and-heart-rate.html

Kotz, Deborah. 2013. Cure for distracted mind: Stare at a painting for three hours. *The Boston Globe.* 27 May 2013.

Kotz, Deborah. 2015. Self affirmations can be good for you. *The Boston Globe.* 21 February 2015.

Krueger, Alan B., and David A. Schkade. 2008. The reliability of subjective well-being measures. *Journal of Public Economics.* August 2008. 92(8-9):1833-1845. https://dx.doi.org/10.1016%2Fj.jpubeco.2007.12.015

Krueger, Alan B., ed. 2009. *Measuring the Subjective Well-Being of Nations: National Accounts of Time Use and Well-Being (National Bureau of Economic Research Conference Report)*. Chicago: University of Chicago Press.
https://www.nber.org/books/krue08-1

Krueger, Alan B., Daniel Kahneman, David Schkade, Norbert Schwarz, and Arthur A. Stone. 2009. National time accounting: The currency of life. *Measuring the Subjective Well-Being of Nations: National Accounts of Time Use and Well-Being (National Bureau of Economic Research Conference Report)*. Chicago: University of Chicago Press.

Ladner, Lorne. 2004. *The Lost Art of Compassion: Discovering the Practice of Happiness in the Meeting of Buddhism and Psychology*. New York: HarperSanFrancisco.

Lakoff, George. 2004, 2014. *The All New Don't Think of an Elephant*. White River Junction, Vermont: Chelsea Green Publishing.

Langer, Ellen. 1989. *Mindfulness*. Philadelphia: Da Capo Press.

Laverty, Luke, Eve A. Edelstein, and Richard Brink. 2016. The sound of creativity: Correlating brainwave and psychometric changes with workplace acoustics. *Proceedings of the Academy of Neuroscience for Architecture 2016 Conference*.
https://www.brikbase.org/content/sound-creativity-correlating-brainwave-psychometric-changes-workplace-acoustics

Layne, Jennifer E., and Miriam E. Nelson. 1999. The effects of progressive resistance training on bone density: A review. *Medicine and Science in Sports and Exercise*. January 1999. 31(1):25-30.
https://doi.org/10.1097/00005768-199901000-00006

Lee, J. J., E. S. Jin, L. K. Rice, and R. A. Josephs. 2015. Hormones and ethics: Understanding the biological basis of unethical conduct. *Journal of Experimental Psychology: General*. 27 July 2015. 144(5):891-897.
https://doi.org/10.1037/xge0000099

Lesiuk, Teresa. 2005. The effect of music listening on work performance. *Psychology of Music*. 1 April 2005. 33(2):173-191.
https://doi.org/10.1177%2F0305735605050650

Lewis, Kevin. 2012. Uncommon Knowledge: Cut yourself some slack. *The Boston Globe*. 10 June 2012.

Lewis, Kevin. 2013. Uncommon Knowledge: How to demotivate white people. *The Boston Globe*. 3 February 2013.

Lewis, Kevin. 2014. Uncommon Knowledge: Belief in self-control makes it real. *The Boston Globe*. 19 October 2014.

Lewis, Kevin. 2014. Uncommon Knowledge: A big healthy rainbow of feelings. *The Boston Globe*. 19 October 2014.

Lewis, Kevin. 2014. Uncommon Knowledge: Ouch! I feel lonely. *The Boston Globe*. 13 July 2014.

Lewis, Kevin. 2014. Uncommon Knowledge: Start with the small stuff. *The Boston Globe*. 1 June 2014.

Lewis, Kevin. 2014. Uncommon Knowledge: The glee of 'ee' and the woe of 'oh'. *The Boston Globe*. 20 April 2014.

Lewis, Kevin. 2014. Uncommon Knowledge: The 'I can change' effect. *The Boston Globe*. 6 July 2014.

Lewis, Kevin. 2014. Uncommon Knowledge: The rice-wheat divide. *The Boston Globe*. 1 June 2014.

Lewis, Kevin. 2014. Uncommon Knowledge: Uncertain? Pat this. *The Boston Globe*. 11 May 2014.

Lewis, Kevin. 2015. Uncommon Knowledge: Forgive, and leap high. *The Boston Globe*. 18 January 2015.

Lewis, Kevin. 2015. Uncommon Knowledge: Searching for sadness. *The Boston Globe*. 5 July 2015.

Lewis, Kevin. 2016. Uncommon Knowledge: Lean in – to yourself. *The Boston Globe*. 7 August 2016.

Lidsky, Theodore, I. 2014. Is the Aluminum Hypothesis dead? *Journal of Occupational and Environmental Medicine*. 8 May 2014. 56(5 Suppl):S73-S79.
https://dx.doi.org/10.1097%2FJOM.0000000000000063

Lyubomirsky, Sonja, Kennon M. Sheldon, and David Schkade. 2005. Pursuing happiness: The architecture of sustainable change. *Review of General Psychology*. June 2005. 9(2):111-131.

Lyubomirsky, Sonja. 2007. *The How of Happiness: A New Approach to Getting the Life You Want*. New York: The Penguin Press.

Maguire, Eleanor A., Katherine Woollett, and Hugo J. Spiers. 2006. London taxi drivers and bus drivers: A structural MRI and neuropsychological analysis. *Hippocampus*. 5 October 2006. 16(12):1091-1101.
https://doi.org/10.1002/hipo.20233

Maizels, Morris, Andrew Blumenfeld, and Raoul Burchette. 2004. A combination of riboflavin, magnesium, and feverfew for migraine prophylaxis: A randomized trial. *Headache: The Journal of Head and Face Pain*. November 2004. 44(9):885-890.
https://www.researchgate.net/publication/8266944_A_Combination_of_Riboflavin_Magnesium_and_Feverfew_for_Migraine_Prophylaxis_A_R andomized_Trial

Mandela, Nelson. 1995. *The Long Walk to Freedom: The Autobiography of Nelson Mandela*. New York: Back Bay Books.

Manson, Mark. 2016. *The Subtle Art of Not Giving a F*ck: A Counterintuitive Approach to Living a Good Life*. New York: HarperCollins.

Martorell, Anthony J., Abigail L. Paulson, Ho-Jun Suk, Fatema Abdurrob, Gabrielle T. Drummond, Webster Guan, Jennie Z. Young, David Nam-Woo Kim, Oleg Kritskiy, Scarlett J. Barker, Vamsi Mangena, Stephanie M. Prince, Emery N. Brown, Kwanghun Chung, Deward S. Boyden, Annabelle C. Singer, and Li-Huei Tsai. 2019. Multi-sensory gamma stimulation ameliorates Alzheimer's-associated pathology and improves cognition. *Cell*. 4 April 2019. 177:256-271.
https://www.cell.com/cell/pdf/S0092-8674(19)30163-1.pdf

Mauss, Iris, B., Maya Tamir, Craig L. Anderson, and Nicole S. Savino. 2011. Can seeking happiness make people unhappy? Paradoxical effects of valuing happiness. *Emotion*. August 2011. 11(4):807-815. https://psycnet.apa.org/doi/10.1037/a0022010

Mayo Clinic. 2019. Strength training: Get stronger, leaner, healthier. *Mayo Clinic*. 23 February 2019. https://www.mayoclinic.org/healthy-lifestyle/fitness/in-depth/strength-training/art-20046670

McGraw, Tim. 2006. When the Stars Go Blue. On *Tim McGraw Reflected: Greatest Hits Volume 2*. Curb Records.

McRaven, William H., Admiral (Ret.). 2017. *Make Your Bed: Little Things That Can Change Your Life… And Maybe the World*. New York: Grand Central Publishing.

Mehta, Ravi, Rui (Juliet) Zhu, and Amar Cheema. 2012. Is noise always bad? Exploring the effects of ambient noise on creative cognition. *Journal of Consumer Research*. December 2012. 39(4):784-799. https://www.jstor.org/stable/10.1086/665048?seq=1#metadata_info_tab_contents

Mendes, Shawn. 2018. In My Blood. On *Shawn Mendes: The Album*. Island Records. https://youtu.be/36tggrpRoTI

Millgram, Yael, Jutta Joormann, Jonathan D. Huppert, and Maya Tamir. 2015. Sad as a matter of choice? Emotion-regulation goals in depression. *Psychological Science*. 19 June 2015. 26(8):1216-1228. https://doi.org/10.1177%2F0956797615583295

Mischkowski, Dominic, Jennifer Crocker, and Baldwin M. Way. From painkiller to empathy killer: Acetaminophen (paracetamol) reduces empathy for pain. *Social Cognitive and Affective Neuroscience*. 5 May 2016. 11(9):1345-1353. https://doi.org/10.1093/scan/nsw057

Mohr, Tara S. 2014. Why women don't apply for jobs unless they're 100% qualified. *Harvard Business Review*. 25 August 2014.

https://hbr.org/2014/08/why-women-dont-apply-for-jobs-unless-theyre-100-qualified

Montgomery, Sy. 2015. Your brain on pets. *The Boston Globe*. 12 January 2015.

Mujica-Parodi, Lilianne R., Helmut H. Strey, Blaise Frederick, Robert Savoy, David Cox, Yevgeny Botanov, Denis Tolkunov, Denis Rubin, and Jochen Weber. 2009. Chemosensory cues to conspecific emotional stress activate amygdala in humans. *PLoS ONE*. 29 July 2009. https://doi.org/10.1371/journal.pone.0006415

Munshi, Sarfaraz, M.D. 2020. Doctor Srafaraz Munshi at Queens Hospital in the UK advises on corona virus breathing technique. *YouTube*. 3 April 2020. https://www.youtube.com/watch?v=HwLzAdriec0&feature=youtu.be

Murthy, Vivek H. 2020. *Together: The Healing Power of Human Connection in a Sometimes Lonely World*. New York: Harper Wave.

Nakazawa, Donna Jackson. 2020. *The Angel and the Assassin: The Tiny Brain Cell That Changed the Course of Medicine*. New York: Ballantine Books.

Nakazawa, Donna Jackson. 2020. From lab to clinic: Hope for those suffering from depression. *The Boston Globe*. 21 January 2020.

National Public Radio (NPR). 1994. Mood of country politically/religiously. All Things Considered (Weekend). *NPR*. 2 January 1994.

NPR, and Margot Adler. 2006. Peace activist William Sloane Coffin dies at 81. *NPR*. 13 April 2006. https://www.npr.org/templates/story/story.php?storyId=5339877

Nazish, Noma. 2019. When's the best time to exercise: Morning or evening? *Forbes*. 28 February 2019. https://www.forbes.com/sites/nomanazish/2019/02/28/whens-the-best-time-to-exercise-morning-or-evening/#9767706d3ce4

Newberg, Andrew, M.D., and Mark Waldman. 2012. The most dangerous word in the world. *Psychology Today*. 1 August 2012. https://www.psychologytoday.com/us/blog/words-can-change-your-brain/201208/the-most-dangerous-word-in-the-world

Neyfakh, Leon. 2014. You can't be serious. *The Boston Globe*. 20 July 2014.

Nieuwenhuis, M., Knight, C., Postmes, and S. A. Haslam. 2014. The relative benefits of green versus lean office space: Three field experiments. *Journal of Experimental Psychology: Applied*. September 2014. 20(3):199-214. https://doi.org/10.1037/xap0000024

Noguchi, Yuki. 2020. Enjoy the extra day off! More bosses give 4-day work week a try. *NPR: Morning Edition*. 21 February 2020. https://www.npr.org/2020/02/21/807133509/enjoy-the-extra-day-off-more-bosses-give-4-day-workweek-a-try

Nye, Naomi Shihab. 1995. *Words Under the Words: Selected Poems*. Portland, Oregon: The Eighth Mountain Press.

Oatley, Keith. 2016. Fiction: Simulation of social worlds. 1 August 2016. 20(8):618-628.

Olmert, M. D. 2009. *Made For Each Other: The Biology of the Human-Animal Bond*. Philadelphia: Da Capo Press.

Oppezzo, Marily, and Daniel L. Schwartz. 2014. Give your ideas some legs: The positive effect of walking on creative thinking. *Journal of Experimental Psychology: Learning, Memory, and Cognition*. 21 April 2014. 40(4):1142-1152.

Park, Seong-Hyun, and Richard H. Mattson. 2008. Effects of flowering and foliage plants in hospital rooms on patients recovering from abdominal surgery. *HortTechnology*. January 2008. 18(4):563-568. https://doi.org/10.21273/HORTTECH.18.4.563

Park, Seong-Hyun, and Richard H. Mattson. 2009. Therapeutic influence of plants in hospital rooms on surgical recovery. *HortScience*. February 2009. 44(1):102-105.
https://doi.org/10.21273/HORTSCI.44.1.102

Park, Seong-Hyun, and Richard H. Mattson. 2009. Ornamental indoor plants in hospital rooms enhanced health outcomes of patients recovering from surgery. *The Journal of Alternative and Complementary Medicine*. September 2009. 15(9):975-980.
https://doi.org/10.1089/acm.2009.0075

Peikert, A., C. Wilimzig, and R. Kohne-Volland. 1996. Prophylaxis of migraine with oral magnesium: Results from a prospective, multi-center, placebo-controlled and double-blind randomized study. *Cephalalgia*. June 1996. 16(4):257-263.
https://doi.org/10.1046/j.1468-2982.1996.1604257.x

Pencavel, John. 2014. *The Productivity of Working Hours*. Stanford University and Institute for the Study of Labor (IZA) Discussion Paper Number 8129. Bonn, Germany. April 2014.

Perpetual Guardian, 2019. *The Four-Day Week: Guidelines for an Outcome-Based Trial – Raising Productivity and Engagement*. White Paper, in association with Coulthard Barnes, Perpetual Guardian, The University of Aukland, Aukland University of Technology, and MinterEllisonRuddWatts.

Petersen, Andrea. 2013. Clinic of the future: Aiming for faster depression relief. *The Wall Street Journal*. 25 June 2013.

Pilkey, Dav. 2000. *Captain Underpants and the Perilous Plot of Professor Poopypants*. New York: Scholastic.

Pink, Daniel H. 2010. *RSA Animate: Drive: The Surprising Truth About What Motivates Us*. YouTube Video.
https://youtu.be/u6XAPnuFjJc

Pink, Daniel H. 2011. *Drive: The Surprising Truth About What Motivates Us*. New York: Riverhead Books.

Pinker, Susan. 2014. *The Village Effect: How Face-To-Face Contact Can Make Us Healthier, Happier, and Smarter.* New York: Spiegel and Grau/Random House.

Pinker, Susan. 2015. People who need people have the longest lives. *The Wall Street Journal.* 27 June 2015.

Powell, Colin L., with Tony Koltz. 2012. *It Worked for Me: In Life and Leadership.* New York: HarperCollins Publishers.

Powell, Colin L. 2015. The Sage Conversation Keynote. 28 July 2015. New Orleans: Sage Summit.

Pratt, Katherine Schwarzenegger. 2020. *The Gift of Forgiveness.* Pamela Dorman Books.

Prior, Ryan. 2020. Belly fat in older women is linked to a 39% higher risk of dementia within 15 years, study says. *CNN Health.* 23 June 2020. https://www.cnn.com/2020/06/23/health/belly-fat-dementia-link-wellness/index.html

Psychedelic Furs. 1984. The Ghost in You. On *While We're Young.* Sony Music Entertainment UK Limited. https://youtu.be/T87u5yuUVi8

Quoidbach, Jordi, June Gruber, Moïra Mikolajczak, Alexsandr Kogan, Ilios Kotsou, and Michael I. Norton. 2014. Emodiversity and the emotional ecosystem. *Journal of Experimental Psychology: General.* December 2014. 143(6):2057-2066. https://www.researchgate.net/deref/http%3A%2F%2Fdx.doi.org%2F10.1037%2Fa0038025

Rasch, Björn, and Jan Born. 2013. About sleep's role in memory. *Physiological Reviews.* 1 April 2013. 93(2):681-766. https://doi.org/10.1152/physrev.00032.2012

Rauch, Jonathan. 2014. The real roots of mid-life crisis. *The Atlantic.* December 2014.

Raudenbush, Bryan, Rebecca Grayhem, Tom Sears, and Ian Wilson. 2009. Effects of peppermint and cinnamon odor administration on simulated driving alertness, mood, and workload. *North American Journal of Psychology*. June 2009. 11(2):245-256.
https://pdfs.semanticscholar.org/a771/038157f4117c58c5af02110ff3f784e3 9c00.pdf

Read to a Child. 2020. Why read to a child.
https://readtoachild.org/program/why-read-to-a-child/

Rendon, Jim. 2015. After trauma, scars but also strength. *The Wall Street Journal*. 19 September 2015.

Riggio, Ronald E., Ph.D. 2012. There's magic in your smile: How smiling affects your brain. *Psychology Today*. 25 June 2012.
https://www.psychologytoday.com/us/blog/cutting-edge-leadership/201206/there-s-magic-in-your-smile

Roberts, Jennifer L. 2013. The power of patience: Teaching students the value of deceleration and immersive attention. *Harvard Magazine*. November-December 2013.

Robertson, Sally. 2019. Morning exercise may burn more calories. *News – Medical Life Sciences*. 19 April 2019.
https://www.news-medical.net/news/20190419/Morning-exercise-may-burn-more-calories.aspx

Robinson, Alan G, and Dean M. Schroeder. 2006. *Ideas Are Free: How the Idea Revolution is Liberating People and Transforming Organizations*. San Francisco, CA: Berrett-Koehler Publishers.

Rohan, M. L., R. T. Yamamoto, C. T. Ravichandran; K. R. Cayetano, O. G. Morales, D. P. Olson, G. Vitaliano, S. M. Paul, and B. M. Cohen. Rapid mood-elevating effects of low field magnetic stimulation in depression. *Biological Psychiatry*. 1 August 2014. 76(3):186-193.

Rotz, Roland, and Sarah D. Wright. 2005. *Fidget to Focus: Outwit Your Boredom: Sensory Strategies for Living With ADD*. Lincoln, Nebraska: iUniverse.

Rummer, Ralf, Judith Schweppe, René Schlegelmilch, and Martine Grice. 2014. Mood is linked to vowel type: The role of articulatory movements. *Emotion*. April 2014. 14(2): 246-250.
https://psycnet.apa.org/doi/10.1037/a0035752

Russ, Tom C., Lewis O. J. Killin, Jean Hannah, G. David Batty, Ian J. Deary, and John M. Starr. 2020. Aluminum and fluoride in drinking water in relation to later dementia risk. *The British Journal of Psychiatry*. January 2020. 216(1):29-34.
https://doi.org/10.1192/bjp.2018.287

Salahi, Lara. 2014. Be Well: Hyper-connections in the brain linked to depression. *The Boston Globe*. 1 September 2014.

Salahi, Lara. 2014. Be Well: New brain stimulation technique lifts mood quickly, study shows. *The Boston Globe*. 4 August 2014.

Sato, Shogo, Astrid Linde Basse, Milena Schönke, Siwei Chen, Muntaha Samad, Ali Altintas, Rhianna C. Laker, Emilie Dalbram, Romain Barrès, Pierre Baldi, Jonas T. Treebak, Juleen R. Zierath, and Paolo Sassone-Corsi. 2019. Time of exercise specifies the impact on muscle metabolic pathways and systemic energy homeostasis. *Cell Metabolism*. 2 July 2019. 30(1):92-110.
https://www.sciencedirect.com/science/article/abs/pii/S1550413119301834?via%3Dihub

Schaumberg, Rebecca L., and Francis J. Flynn. 2016. Self-Reliance: A gender perspective on its relationship to Communality and Leadership Evaluations. *Academy of Management Journal*. 22 July 2016. 60(5):1859-1881.
https://journals.aom.org/doi/10.5465/amj.2015.0018

Schmidt, Rosemary A. 2015. We are all immigrants. *Rosebud's Blog*. 11 October 2015.
http://www.gainline.com/2015/10/

Schmidt, Rosemary A. 2015. Challenge yourself! *Rosebud's Blog*. 27 January 2015.
http://www.gainline.com/2015/01/

215

Schmidt, Rosemary A. 2018. Turning toward bids creates better workplace relationships. *The Gottman Institute*. 18 April 2018.
https://www.gottman.com/blog/turning-toward-bids-better-work-relationships/

Scholey, Andrew. 2004. Chewing gum and cognitive performance: A case of functional food with function but no food? *Appetite*. October 2004. 43(2):215-216.
https://doi.org/10.1016/j.appet.2004.07.004

Schönauer, M., S. Alizadeh, H. Jamalabadi, A. Abraham, A. Pawlizki, and S. Gais. 2017. Decoding material-specific memory processing during sleep in humans. *Nature Communications*. 17 May 2017. Article Number 15404.
https://doi.org/10.1038/ncomms15404

Schulte, Brigid. 2015. Do these exercises for two minutes a day and you'll immediately feel happier, researchers say. *The Washington Post*. 29 June 2015.

Seligman, Martin E. P., Ph.D. 1990. *Learned Optimism: How to Change Your Mind and Your Life*. New York: Vintage Books, a Division of Random House, Inc.

Seligman, Martin E. P., Ph.D. 1993. *What You Can Change... And What You Can't: The Complete Guide to Successful Self-Improvement*. New York: Ballantine Books, a division of Random House.

Sertori, J. M. 1998. *The Little Book of Feng Shui*. Bath: Paragon.

Seppälä, Emma. 2016. A Stanford psychologist explains why spacing out and goofing off is so good for you. *The Washington Post*. 2 February 2016.

Shastri, Devi, and Guy Boulton. 2020. Less-invasive breathing therapies could keep 'significant number' of patients off ventilators. *USA Today*. 28 April 2020.
https://www.usatoday.com/story/news/nation/2020/04/27/ventilator-alternatives-show-promise-ease-shortage-fears-coronavirus-covid-19-wisconsin-milwaukee/3033873001/

Shellenbarger, Sue. 2015. Power of tiny distractions. *The Wall Street Journal*. 3 March 2015.

Shellenbarger, Sue. 2015. Work & Family Mail Box: How is stress conveyed from one person to another? *The Wall Street Journal*. 11 March 2015.

Silverman, Rachel Emma. 2014. Men and women at work: Unhappy, but productive. *Wall Street Journal*. 15 December 2014. http://blogs.wsj.com/atwork/2014/12/15/men-and-women-at-work-unhappy-but-productive/

Snow, Catherine E., M. Susan Burns, and Peg Griffin, ed. 1998. *Preventing Reading Difficulties in Young Children*. National Research Council. Washington, D.C.: National Academy Press.

Stanton, Angela A. 2017. *Fighting the Migraine Epidemic: Complete Guide: How to Treat and Prevent Migraines Without Medication*. North Charleston, South Carolina: CreateSpace Independent Publishing Platform.

Steinberg, Stephanie. 2012. Can fans affect whether the Red Sox win or lose? *The Boston Globe*. 31 August 2012.

Stephens, Richard, John Atkins, and Andrew Kingston. 2009. Swearing as a response to pain. *Neuroreport*. August 2009. 20(12):1056-1060.

Stipe, Michael, and Chris Martin. 2006. In the Sun. On *In the Sun Gulf Coast Relief*. Warner-Tamerlane Publishing Corp.

Stone, Arthur A., Joseph E. Schwartz, Joan E. Broderick, and Angus Deaton. 2010. A Snapshot of the Age Distribution of Psychological Well-Being in the United States. *Proceedings of the National Academy of Sciences of the United States of America*. 1 June 1010. 107(22): 9985-9990. https://www.pnas.org/content/107/22/9985

Sugay, Celine. 2019. How to measure happiness with tests and surveys (and quizzes). *Positive Psychology.com*. 19 November 2019. https://positivepsychology.com/measure-happiness-tests-surveys/

Talarovicova, A., L. Krskova, and A. Kiss. 2007. Some assessments of the amygdala role in suprahypothalamic neuroendocrine regulation: A minireview. *Endocrine Regulations*. November 2007. 41(4):155-162.
https://www.ncbi.nlm.nih.gov/pubmed/18257652

Talhelm, T., X. Zhang, S. Oishi, C Shimin, D. Duan, X. Lan, and S. Kitayama. 2014. Large-scale psychological differences within China explained by rice versus wheat agriculture. *Science*. 9 May 2014. 344(6184):603-608.
https://doi.org/10.1126/science.1246850

Tamir, Diana I., Andrew B. Bricker, David Dodell-Feder, and Jason P. Mitchell. 2016. Reading fiction and reading minds: The role of simulation in the default network. *Social Cognitive and Affective Neuroscience*. February 2016. 11(2):215-224.
https://dx.doi.org/10.1093%2Fscan%2Fnsv114

Tamir, Maya, Shalom H. Schwartz, Shige Oishi, and Min Y. Kim. 2017. The secret to happiness: Feeling good or right? *Journal of Experimental Psychology: General*. August 2017. 146(10):1448-1459.
https://www.researchgate.net/deref/http%3A%2F%2Fdx.doi.org%2F10.1037%2Fxge0000303

Tapiainen, V., H. Taipale, A. Tanskanen, J. Tiihonen, S. Hartikainen, and A.-M. Tolppanen. 2018. The risk of Alzheimer's disease associated with benzodiazepines and related drugs: A nested case-control study. *Acta Psychiatrica Scandinavica*. 31 May 2018.

Tarleton, Emily K., Benjamin Littenberg, Charles D. MacLean, Amanda G. Kennedy, and Christopher Daley. 2017. Role of magnesium supplementation in the treatment of depression: A randomized clinical trial. *PLoS ONE*. 27 June 2017.
https://doi.org/10.1371/journal.pone.0180067

Taylor, Jill Bolte, Ph.D. 2008. *My Stroke of Insight: A Brain Scientist's Personal Journey*. New York: Viking Penguin.

Teitell, Beth. 2018. Worrying about sleep keeps us up at night. *The Boston Globe*. 13 April 2018.

The Annie E. Casey Foundation. 2010. *Early Warning! Why Reading By the End of Third Grade Matters: KIDS COUNT Special Report*. Written by Leila Fiester, for The Annie E. Casey Foundation. Baltimore, Maryland.

The Annie E. Casey Foundation. 2013. *Early Warning Confirmed: A Research Update on Third-Grade Reading*. Written by Leila Fiester, for The Annie E. Casey Foundation. Baltimore, Maryland.

Towles, Amor. 2016. *A Gentleman in Moscow*. New York: Penguin Random House.

Toyoda, Masahiro, Yuko Yukota, Marni Barnes, and Midori Kaneko. 2019. Potential for a small plant on the desk for reducing office workers' stress. *HortTechnology*. 9 December 2019. 30(1):55-63. https://doi.org/10.21273/HORTTECH04427-19

Ueland, Brenda. 1938. *If You Want To Write: A Book About Art, Independence, and Spirit*. Saint Paul, Minnesota: Graywolf Press.

Ulrich, R. S. 1984. View through a window may influence recovery from surgery. *Science*. April 1984. 224(4647):420-421. https://doi.org/10.1126/science.6143402

University of Exeter. 2014. Why plants in the office make us more productive. *Science Daily*. 1 September 2014. https://www.sciencedaily.com/releases/2014/09/140901090735.htm

Van der Kolk, Bessel. 2014. *The Body Keeps the Score: Brain, Mind, and Body in the Healing of Trauma*. New York: Penguin Books.

Van der Kolk, Bessel, as told to Rachel Deahl. 2014. Getting past hurt. *The Boston Globe*. 14 September 2014.

Van Horen, Femke, and Thomas Mussweiler. 2014. Soft assurance: Coping with uncertainty through haptic sensations. *Journal of Experimental Social Psychology*. September 2014. 54:73-80. https://doi.org/10.1016/j.jesp.2014.04.008

Vink, Robert, and Mihai Nechifor, editors. 2011. *Magnesium in the Central Nervous System*. Adelaide, South Australia: University of Adelaide Press.
https://doi.org/10.1017/UPO9780987073051

Wahl, Erik. 2013. *Unthink: Rediscover Your Creative Genius*. New York: Crown Business.

Waldinger, Robert. 2015. What makes a good life? Lessons from the longest study on happiness. *TEDxBeaconStreet*. November 2015.
https://www.ted.com/talks/robert_waldinger_what_makes_a_good_life_lessons_from_the_longest_study_on_happiness?utm_campaign=tedspread&utm_medium=referral&utm_source=tedcomshare

Walker, Matthew P., and Robert Stickgold. 2006. Sleep, memory, and plasticity. *Annual Review of Psychology*. 10 January 2006. 57:139-166.
https://doi.org/10.1146/annurev.psych.56.091103.070307

Warm, Joel S., William N. Dember, and Raja Parasuraman. 1991. Effects of olfactory stimulation on performance and stress in a visual sustained attention task. *Journal of the Society of Cosmetic Chemists*. January 1991.
https://www.researchgate.net/publication/238116157_Effects_of_olfactory_stimulation_on_performance_and_stress_in_a_visual_sustained_attention_task

Warren, Jane E., Disa A. Sauter, Frank Eisner, Jade Wiland, M. Alexander Dresner, Richard J. S. Wise, Stuart Rosen, and Sophie K. Scott. 2006. Positive emotions preferentially engage an auditory-motor "mirror" system. *The Journal of Neuroscience*. 13 December 2006. 26(50):13067-13075.
https://doi.org/10.1523/JNEUROSCI.3907-06.2006

Waters, Sara F., Tessa V. West, and Wendy Berry Mendes. 2014. Stress contagion: Covariation between mothers and infants. *Psychological Science*. 1 April 2014. 25(4):934-942.
https://dx.doi.org/10.1177%2F0956797613518352

Weintraub, Karen. 2014. Daylight savings time may be hazardous to your health. *USA Today*. 7 March 2014.

Weintraub, Karen. 2015. Stress may make you more likely to cheat. *The Boston Globe*. 15 August 2015.

Williams, Lawrence E, and John A. Bargh. 2008. Experiencing physical warmth promotes interpersonal warmth. *Science*. 24 October 2008. 322(5901):606-607.
https://doi.org/10.1126/science.1162548

Wilson, Timothy D., David A. Reinhard, Erin C. Westgate, Daniel T. Gilbert, Nicole Ellerbeck, Cheryl Hahn, Casey L. Brown, and Adi Shaked. 2014. Just think: The challenges of the disengaged mind. *Science*. 4 July 2014. 345(6192):75-77.
https://dx.doi.org/10.1126%2Fscience.1250830

Wood, Adrienne, Magdalena Rychlowska, Sebastian Korb, and Paula Niedenthal. 2016. Fashioning the face: Sensorimotor simulation contributes to facial expression recognition. *Trends in Cognitive Science*. 11 February 2016. 20(3):227-240.
https://doi.org/10.1016/j.tics.2015.12.010

Yeager, David Scott, Rebecca Johnson, Brian James Spitzer, Kali H. Trzesniewski, Joseph Powers, and Carol S. Dweck. 2014. The far-reaching effects of believing people can change: Implicit theories of personality shape stress, health, and achievement during adolescence. *Journal of Personality and Social Psychology*. June 2014. 106(6):867-884.
https://psycnet.apa.org/doi/10.1037/a0036335

Yong, Ed. 2010. Heavy, rough and hard – how the things we touch affect our judgments and decisions. *Discover Magazine*. 25 June 2010.
http://blogs.discovermagazine.com/notrocketscience/2010/06/25/heavy-rough-and-hard-how-the-things-we-touch-affect-our-judgments-and-decisions/#.XFnL3eRYaUn

Zheng, Xue, Ryan Fehr, Kenneth Tai, Jayanth Narayanan, and Michele J. Gelfand. 2014. The unburdening effects of forgiveness. *Social Psychological and Personality Science*. 23 December 2014.
https://doi.org/10.1177%2F1948550614564222

Additional Suggested Reading on Happiness:

Happier, by Tal Ben-Shahar.

Happiness Now, by Robert Holden, PhD.

The Happiness Curve: Why Life Gets Better After 50, by Jonathan Rauch.

Index

Cover Art & Fonts

The image on the cover is a painting by Carol Aust, titled *Fearless*. I found it at the Left Bank Gallery, in Wellfleet, Massachusetts, back in 2015. I'd gone to visit a friend in town there, and as we walked, wandering in and out of galleries, I saw this painting and I absolutely fell in love with it, with its delicious blue sky and leap of faith. I'm thrilled now to be able to share it with the world. To see more of Carol Aust's work, visit: www.carolaust.com.

The painting was photographed by Scot Langdon of Long Hill Photography, a true professional and a real hero in time of need.

The fonts used on the front cover are from the Goodlife family of fonts, designed by Hannes von Döhren in 2015, offered by HVD Fonts, a Berlin-based foundry. It features beautifully hand-drawn lettering, blending cursive script with brush strokes, for a humanistic hand-crafted feel.

The spiral on the back cover is from the GoodDog font family, designed by Ethan Dunham of the Fonthead foundry in Wilmington, Delaware, and is an ancient symbol of healing and the journey of life.

The text on the back cover is set in Agenda, designed by Greg Thompson. The interior text of the book is set in Palatino Linotype. Chapter headings are Lucida Sans.

The author photo was taken by Susan C. Lurier. The photo of the clam was taken at Nantasket Beach, in Hull, Massachusetts.

About the Author

Rose Schmidt is a writer, sometimes poet, philosopher, publisher, and blogger, covering the range of human experience, from art and music to science and psychology. She has retired from playing rugby, and clearly spends a lot of time thinking. Rose grew up in Aurora, Illinois, attended the University of Dayton, and University of Illinois, and resides with her spouse, Susan, in the Boston area.

Also by Rose:

Go Forward, Support! The Rugby of Life

Rosebud's Blog:
www.RosebudsBlog.com
www.happyclam.net

GAINLINE PRESS
P.O. Box 1166
Watertown, Massachusetts 02471
www.gainline.com

Made in the USA
Las Vegas, NV
27 March 2022

46399598R10142